GOD GRANT ME...

Peace that Replaces Worry

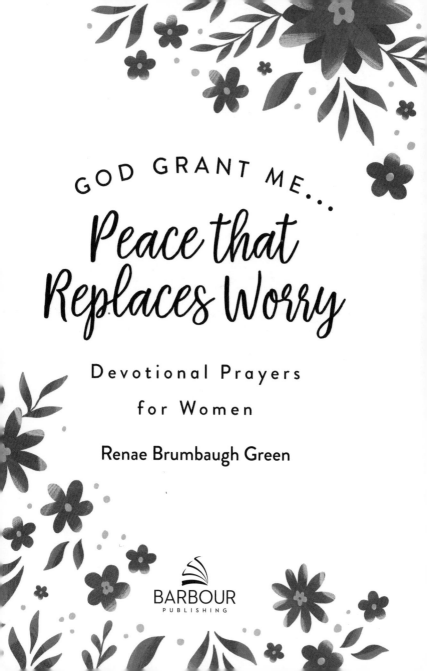

GOD GRANT ME...

Peace that Replaces Worry

Devotional Prayers
for Women

Renae Brumbaugh Green

BARBOUR
PUBLISHING

Print ISBN 978-1-63609-495-3

Cover Design: Greg Jackson, Thinkpen Design

Published by Barbour Publishing, Inc., 1810 Barbour Drive, Uhrichsville, Ohio 44683, www.barbourbooks.com

Our mission is to inspire the world with the life-changing message of the Bible.

Member of the
Evangelical Christian
Publishers Association

Printed in China.

Introduction

For many of us, we treat worry like it's a stray pet. We feed it, water it, nurture it. . .and we wonder why it won't go away. But God didn't create us for worry. Worry is simply a manifestation of fear. It's the belief that something bad will happen. Time and again in His Word, God tells us not to be afraid. Instead, we're to have hope, which is the opposite of fear. Hope is the belief that good things are coming. And God calls Himself the God of hope.

So how do we stop worrying when worry is so familiar and comfortable it's like a member of the family? The key to removing worry from our lives is to replace it with something else. We must crowd it out so there's no room left in the inn of our hearts. When we're tempted to worry, we need to pray. When fear creeps in, we should praise God. When anxiety steals our sleep, we can sing every praise song we know. After all, God lives in our praise. And where God is, there's no room for fear of any kind.

*Don't worry about anything, but pray and ask
God for everything you need, always giving thanks
for what you have. And because you belong to
Christ Jesus, God's peace will stand guard over
all your thoughts and feelings. His peace can
do this far better than our human minds.*

PHILIPPIANS 4:6–7 ERV

Default Setting

Our soul waits for the LORD; he is our help and
our shield. For our heart is glad in him, because
we trust in his holy name. Let your steadfast love,
O LORD, be upon us, even as we hope in you.
PSALM 33:20–22 ESV

. . . .

Dear Father, what a beautiful prayer. The psalmist waited for You, was glad in You, trusted You, and found hope in You. What did this psalmist have that I don't? I want to be in that place, Lord. I want to rest in You, knowing You'll take care of me. But I'm not there. No matter how I try to trust Your goodness, my default setting goes to fear. Hope is the opposite of fear, isn't it? Hope is the belief that something good will happen, while fear is the belief that something bad will happen. Give me the strength and self-discipline to change my default setting. You're the God of hope, which means You have good things in store for my life. Help me believe that, Lord.

Comparison

And Salmon the father of Boaz by Rahab,
and Boaz the father of Obed by Ruth,
and Obed the father of Jesse.

MATTHEW 1:5 ESV

Dear Father, much of my worry and anxiety happens because I compare myself to others. I look at the perfect, public versions of their lives and feel I don't measure up. I look at my past and my imperfections and worry that I'll never be good enough. This verse is a powerful reminder that You choose—and use—imperfect people with sketchy pasts. Rahab was a prostitute, yet You chose her to be one of Jesus' great-grandmothers. Ruth was from Moab, and Moabites were typically despised by Jews. Yet You chose her, as well, to be a grandmother to Your Son. Thank You for the peace that comes from knowing that no matter what my past looks like, no matter how imperfect I may seem, You have chosen me. Use me as You will, Father.

Consistent

Now the birth of Jesus Christ took place in this way. When his mother Mary had been betrothed to Joseph, before they came together she was found to be with child from the Holy Spirit.

MATTHEW 1:18 ESV

. . . .

Dear Father, a virgin, carrying Your Son? That doesn't make sense. Yet Your Word prophesied of just such a virgin birth centuries before it happened. Your ways don't always make sense to me, Father. I often stress myself out trying to make sense of things, but that's pointless. I know Your thoughts are far above my own. My circumstances may not always make sense, but I know You will never contradict Your Word. When I worry about the future or question Your leading, remind me to study the Bible. You're consistent, and You won't ever lead me to do something against Your ways. Thank You for the peace that comes from reading Your Word.

God with Us

"Behold, the virgin shall conceive and bear a son, and they shall call his name Immanuel."
MATTHEW 1:23 ESV

Dear Father, the name Immanuel means "God with us." It amazes me that You, the King of kings, chose to be with us. We were awful to You. We disobeyed You. We were rebellious. Still, You chose to come down here and live among us. So often, Satan tries to tell me I've blown it with You. He tries to convince me that *my* sins are too great, *my* mistakes too catastrophic for You to want me. In my head, I know Satan lies to me. But in my heart, his lies ring true. Thank You for Your Word that tells me Satan's a liar. Thank You for this reminder that You wanted me. In all Your glory, You chose to be with me. And thank You for the knowledge that nothing I do can ever change Your love for me.

Wise Men

Now after Jesus was born in Bethlehem of Judea in the days of Herod the king, behold, wise men from the east came to Jerusalem, saying, "Where is he who has been born king of the Jews? For we saw his star when it rose and have come to worship him."

MATTHEW 2:1–2 ESV

Dear Father, so many of my days are spent worrying about whether I'm doing the right things and making the good choices. But You replace worry with peace! You promise wisdom to whoever asks for it. These wise men are a great example of how to be wise in a world of fools. First, wisdom seeks to worship You. Am I doing that each day? I want to, Lord. Next, wisdom follows You and rejects earthly things. Help me reject the habit of worry and trust You. Finally, wisdom gives precious gifts to You. Am I giving You my best? Thank You for these reminders, Father. I want the peace that comes with Your wisdom.

Doing My Best

Going into the house, they saw the child with Mary his mother, and they fell down and worshiped him. Then, opening their treasures, they offered him gifts, gold and frankincense and myrrh.

MATTHEW 2:11 ESV

. . . .

Dear Father, I sometimes wonder if Mary thought, "I would have rather been given diapers." These men gave Your Son the best they had. They didn't worry about whether they should be doing more or if their gifts were appropriate. They found great purpose in simply giving their best. Too often, I overthink things. I worry that what I'm doing isn't the right thing or that it's not good enough or not appropriate. But if I'm giving my best and doing all I can to honor You, it's right, and You are pleased. The question is, am I truly giving my best—my time, my resources, my talents—as gifts to You? I want to, Lord. Thank You for helping me find joy and purpose in simply being myself and doing my best.

Final Say

Then Herod, when he saw that he had been tricked by the wise men, became furious, and he sent and killed all the male children in Bethlehem and in all that region who were two years old or under, according to the time that he had ascertained from the wise men.
MATTHEW 2:16 ESV

. . . .

Dear Father, Satan is evil. He wants to destroy our lives. In this case, Satan worked through Herod. But Satan did not have the final say! Jesus survived, and Your plan for our salvation continued. I know Satan wants to destroy my life as well. He uses worry, fear, and anxiety to paralyze me and suck the joy out of my existence. But he won't have the final say. I know Your plans for me are good, and Your purpose for my life includes freedom from worry. Remind me of that when Satan tries to pull me in. As hard as he may try, he will not win.

Honey and Locusts

John wore a garment of camel's hair and a leather belt around his waist, and his food was locusts and wild honey. Then Jerusalem and all Judea and all the region about the Jordan were going out to him, and they were baptized by him in the river Jordan, confessing their sins.

MATTHEW 3:4–6 ESV

Dear Father, John didn't worry about wealth. He didn't even worry about what he'd eat. He wore rags and ate bugs, but he had a tremendous impact on Your kingdom. He didn't concern himself with earthly things, and yet You cared so tenderly for his needs. After all, honey is considered a delicacy. I'll bet he's wearing some fancy robes now and eating a King's feast! Help me push aside my temporary worries and trust Your goodness. Today, I'll enjoy the honey You send. I look forward to the day I too will wear a robe and dine in Your presence.

Let God Shine

*Then Jesus came from Galilee to the Jordan
to John, to be baptized by him. John would have
prevented him, saying, "I need to be baptized by
you, and do you come to me?" But Jesus answered
him, "Let it be so now, for thus it is fitting for us
to fulfill all righteousness." Then he consented.*
MATTHEW 3:13–15 ESV

Dear Father, one of John's greatest character traits was his humility. He knew his place in comparison to the God of the universe. He never wanted to outshine Christ or receive the attention or glory for himself. In a way, when I worry about things, I forget my place. When I worry, I lack humility. Worry shows that I lack confidence in You and that I think my way is best. Forgive me for that, Father. Give me John's humility to step aside, trust Your goodness, and let You shine.

15

The Sword

Then Jesus was led up by the Spirit into the wilderness to be tempted by the devil. And after fasting forty days and forty nights, he was hungry. And the tempter came and said to him, "If you are the Son of God, command these stones to become loaves of bread." But he answered, "It is written, 'Man shall not live by bread alone, but by every word that comes from the mouth of God.'"

MATTHEW 4:1–4 ESV

Dear Father, Jesus overcame temptation by quoting Your Word. I know it's the same for me. The more of Your Word I know, the easier it will be for me to say no to Satan, to evil thoughts, and to the worrisome lies that take my thoughts captive. Your Word is a living, active thing. It's not just words on a page. Your Word has power! No wonder it's called the sword. Remind me to carry my sword today. When I'm tempted to worry, bring Your Word to mind, and fill me with Your peace.

Practical Needs

*He went throughout all Galilee, teaching
in their synagogues and proclaiming the
gospel of the kingdom and healing every
disease and every affliction among the people.*
MATTHEW 4:23 ESV

Dear Father, Jesus was a teacher. He proclaimed the good news that You love people and want a relationship with them. But He was so much more than a lecturer. He truly loved people and had compassion on them. He met their practical needs. I know Your love hasn't changed ever since Jesus walked the earth. You love me. You see every need, and You care. Whatever my affliction—physical, emotional, financial, or something else—You will see me through it. I don't need to worry about how I'll handle any situation, because I know You already have it handled. You will supply all my needs. Thank You for being a hands-on, practical-needs kind of God. You are amazing, and I love You.

Blessed

He opened his mouth and taught them, saying:
"Blessed are the poor in spirit, for theirs is
the kingdom of heaven. Blessed are those
who mourn, for they shall be comforted."
MATTHEW 5:2–4 ESV

Dear Father, these verses begin a list of promises to Your children. And I know You always keep Your promises. For each difficult thing we endure here on earth, You will bless us. When I'm sad, but I trust You, I'm blessed. When I face hard things, but I trust You for the outcome, You add it to my account and I'm blessed. If there's one thing I'm learning about You, Father, it's that You love to bless Your children. Help me take my eyes off the things that cause fear and anxiety and set my eyes on Your promises. I know I don't need to worry about anything. No matter what happens, You've got it covered. I am blessed.

Perfect Like My Father

"If you love those who love you, what reward do you have? Do not even the tax collectors do the same? And if you greet only your brothers, what more are you doing than others? Do not even the Gentiles do the same? You therefore must be perfect, as your heavenly Father is perfect."
MATTHEW 5:46–48 ESV

Dear Father, this command for Your children to be perfect like You. . .that's a tall order. How can I ever be like You? I am sinful. Even when I try my best, I'm often overcome with worries and fears and doubts about myself and the world around me. Yet I know this verse doesn't define the word *perfect* as "without sin." You know I'm human. You know my tendencies, and You love me anyway. You want me to be pure hearted. You want my utmost desire to be for You. I love You, Father. More than anything, I want to please You. Make me pure hearted just like You.

In Secret

"When you give to the needy, sound no trumpet before you, as the hypocrites do in the synagogues and in the streets, that they may be praised by others. Truly, I say to you, they have received their reward. But when you give to the needy, do not let your left hand know what your right hand is doing, so that your giving may be in secret. And your Father who sees in secret will reward you."

MATTHEW 6:2–4 ESV

Dear Father, I like when people notice the things I do for them. I like to be acknowledged. I worry that if people don't know I'm doing these good things, they won't like me. Doing righteous, good deeds in secret, with no one acknowledging or saying "thank you," takes humility. Humility is one of Your favorite traits, isn't it? Truly, if You know about the good things I do, why should I worry about what others think? Thank You for the peace and freedom that comes from pleasing You alone.

All I Need

*"Ask, and it will be given to you; seek, and you
will find; knock, and it will be opened to you. For
everyone who asks receives, and the one who seeks
finds, and to the one who knocks it will be opened."*
MATTHEW 7:7–8 ESV

. . . .

Dear Father, I know You long to give good things to us when we live for You and when we ask in faith. But You know better than I do what is good and what isn't. Sometimes You don't give me what I ask for if the outcome won't be good or won't turn out well for me. I trust Your love for me. I know You will give me everything required to live an abundant, joy-filled, peace-filled life. I know You'll provide all I need to live out Your purpose for me. You know the desires of my heart, Lord. Today, I ask You to fulfill all those longings or change my heart to match what You want for me.

In the End

And he said to them, "Why are you afraid, O you of little faith?" Then he rose and rebuked the winds and the sea, and there was a great calm.
MATTHEW 8:26 ESV

. . . .

Dear Father, I am so much like those disciples. I say I trust You, but when the winds kick up and the storms rage, I get scared. My whole body tenses up, my stomach clenches, and I head into fight-or-flight mode, all before I call out to You. Yet You've never given me reason to doubt Your goodness. I know You will protect me. Even if the storms knock me around, You'll stay with me through it all and You'll carry me through. You've also given me every weapon I need to fight the good fight. When I trust You, use Your Word as my weapon, and face adversity with faith, I know that in the end I'll be the one standing.

The Big Picture

And he said to them, "Go." So they came out and went into the pigs, and behold, the whole herd rushed down the steep bank into the sea and drowned in the waters. The herdsmen fled, and going into the city they told everything, especially what had happened to the demon-possessed men. And behold, all the city came out to meet Jesus, and when they saw him, they begged him to leave their region.
MATTHEW 8:32–34 ESV

Dear Father, Jesus had just performed a miracle. He had changed a life. Yet these herdsmen were more concerned about their pigs than about that man. They begged Jesus to leave because of what He did. They worried about the fiscal impact of this miracle and failed to see the bigger picture. I do the same thing sometimes. Forgive me for worrying about temporary things. Give me Your vision and help me see the big picture.

23

Christ Alone

*When he entered the house, the blind men came
to him, and Jesus said to them, "Do you believe
that I am able to do this?" They said to him,
"Yes, Lord." Then he touched their eyes, saying,
"According to your faith be it done to you."*

MATTHEW 9:28–29 ESV

Dear Father, these men looked for Jesus. They followed Him. They hounded Him to do what they asked. They knew that Christ alone could restore their sight. Why is it that I often use You as a last resort? I try everything I can think of to solve my problems, and when my attempts fail, I seek You. But You are the solution to every problem. Build my faith, Father. When I face any difficulty, large or small, remind me to seek You first. I trust You alone to heal every broken part of me.

Focus Outward

*"Heal the sick, raise the dead, cleanse
lepers, cast out demons. You received
without paying; give without pay."*
MATTHEW 10:8 ESV

Dear Father, Jesus gave His disciples authority to do all the things He did, and He sent them forth. His purpose for their lives was outward focused. He basically said, "Go find people who are sick and needy and hurting, and help them." Too much of my life is spent focusing inward. I worry about things going on in my own life or in the lives of my immediate circle. When I shift my attention to others' needs, it helps them, and it helps me too. Concentrating on helping others gets me out of my head, pushes aside worry and fear, and builds my confidence and faith as I live out Your purpose for my life. Show me people who need Your touch today, Lord, and help me meet their needs.

The Yoke

"Take my yoke upon you, and learn from me, for I am gentle and lowly in heart, and you will find rest for your souls. For my yoke is easy, and my burden is light."
MATTHEW 11:29–30 ESV

Dear Father, I know a yoke is a wooden piece designed for cattle or oxen. It holds the animals together to maximize their effort as they pull a load. A good animal owner will carve each side of the yoke to fit a specific animal. If the yoke doesn't fit well, it will rub and chafe. When You say Your yoke is easy and Your burden is light, You don't mean I won't have a burden. Instead, I can be confident that, with You as my Master, I'll have a yoke that is made to fit me. When I trust You, I'm able to carry my burden with ease. I know You're walking beside me, connected to me, helping me shoulder the load.

The Accuser

*But when the Pharisees saw it, they said to
him, "Look, your disciples are doing what
is not lawful to do on the Sabbath."*
MATTHEW 12:2 ESV

. . . .

Dear Father, the Pharisees watched Jesus. Like predators, they waited for a moment to pounce. They wanted to find fault with Jesus and His disciples so they could arrest them. The disciples were hungry, and they picked a snack from a field on the Sabbath. But Your way is always filled with grace, isn't it? Instead of looking for flaws, You look for ways to show love. Satan, on the other hand, is the accuser. Forgive me for ever aligning myself with Satan. Sometimes I get so worried about the way I think things should be that I look for faults in others. I accuse and try to manipulate instead of showering them with Your love. Make me like You, Father, because I know Your way is better for me and for those around me.

All That Matters

He answered, "Every plant that my heavenly
Father has not planted will be rooted up."
MATTHEW 15:13 ESV

Dear Father, Jesus had just told the crowds that what goes into our mouths doesn't defile us; instead, it's the stuff that comes out of our mouths that reflects what's in our hearts. Food and drink don't make us sinful. . .our thoughts do. When the disciples told Jesus that the religious leaders were offended, He said, "Let it go. Don't worry about what they think. They're not aligned with God's Word, and in the end, their words and actions don't mean a thing." Father, I do worry about what others think and say about me. But in the end, those who don't honor You will be destroyed. What they think doesn't matter at all. Remind me that the only opinion that matters is Yours. Teach me to focus on pleasing You and to disregard everything else.

Safe Place

*He said, "Come." So Peter got out of the boat
and walked on the water and came to Jesus.*
MATTHEW 14:29 ESV

Dear Father, this makes a great story. But if it had been me, I'm not sure I would have stepped out of that boat into the stormy sea. Why did Peter choose to leave his safe place for the dangerous waves? He did it because he had faith. He stepped out of the boat because that's where Jesus was. As long as Peter's eyes stayed focused on Christ, he was unharmed. It was only when Peter moved his focus from Jesus to the storm that he began to sink. Even then, Jesus saved him. Help me have Peter's faith. Help me get out of my comfort zone. No matter what logic may tell me, I know I'm always safest wherever You are—even in the middle of the storm. When I worry, when I shift my focus to my surroundings, gently pull my eyes back to You.

Inheritance

"I will give you the keys of the kingdom of heaven, and whatever you bind on earth shall be bound in heaven, and whatever you loose on earth shall be loosed in heaven."

MATTHEW 16:19 ESV

Dear Father, these words can be hard to understand. Does this mean I have heavenly power and whatever I say will happen? I think that's exactly what this says. . .as long as I'm close to You, as long as I'm in Your perfect will. I can't command things to happen that go against Your plan. You won't allow me to be selfish with the power You've given me. But I can have confidence in knowing that when I believe—when I have faith in You—Your power supports me. Your Word is a mighty weapon. When I speak Your Word and claim Your promises, amazing things happen. I am Your daughter, so of course You've given me the keys to the kingdom and everything within. Thank You for my inheritance. Remind me of Your power in me.

Like a Child

*"Whoever humbles himself like this child is
the greatest in the kingdom of heaven."*
MATTHEW 18:4 ESV

. . . .

Dear Father, that word, *humble*, goes against everything in human nature. Our society teaches us to be assertive and confident. It teaches us to fight for what we want and to try to be the best. It's in our DNA to put ourselves first, to look out for number one. But a little child is humble. A child is totally dependent on her parents for all of life's necessities. You want me to be humble like that, don't You? You want me to be entirely dependent on You for care and support. You want me to relax, knowing You will provide. Forgive me for not depending on You, Father. I'm sorry for my lack of humility. Right now, in this moment, I choose to set my worries aside and trust You completely. I know You will take care of me.

Like a Mustard Seed

When the disciples saw it, they marveled, saying, "How did the fig tree wither at once?" And Jesus answered them, "Truly, I say to you, if you have faith and do not doubt, you will not only do what has been done to the fig tree, but even if you say to this mountain, 'Be taken up and thrown into the sea,' it will happen. And whatever you ask in prayer, you will receive, if you have faith."

MATTHEW 21:20–22 ESV

Dear Father, how strong is my faith? Where does my trust end? Too often, it stops where my problems begin. At the first sign of trouble, my anxiety kicks up, worry sets in, and I forget to trust You. Give me faith the size of a mustard seed, Father, and cause it to grow. Make me strong in You. I know You are always with me, fighting for me. I trust You completely.

Your Will Be Done

And going a little farther he fell on his
face and prayed, saying, "My Father, if it
be possible, let this cup pass from me;
nevertheless, not as I will, but as you will."

MATTHEW 26:39 ESV

. . . .

Dear Father, Jesus knew He was going to die. If anyone had a reason to be afraid, to worry about what was coming, He did. And He *was* afraid. But He didn't let His fear control Him. He asked You to change the course of events. . . but He ended His request by saying, "I want what You want." Thank You for this reminder that it's okay to feel emotions, whatever they may be. It's okay to feel fear and anxiety as long as I don't let those feelings control my actions. Teach me to act in spite of my worry, not because of it. I want what You want, Father, and I trust Your love for me. May Your will be done.

Cast Them Out

And he healed many who were sick with various diseases, and cast out many demons. And he would not permit the demons to speak, because they knew him.

MARK 1:34 ESV

Dear Father, I know Your power still heals the sick and casts out demons. I ask, with faith please cast out any sickness, disease, addictions, relationship issues—anything that is not of You; please throw these out of my life and the lives of those I love. Just as You would not allow the demons to speak in this story, I pray You'll silence these negative situations in my life. Silence the voices in my head that cause me to doubt Your goodness, Your power, and Your love. Thank You for the wonderful things I know You have in store for all those who love You. I love You, I trust You, and I know You are good.

All My Needs

And his disciples answered him, "How can one feed these people with bread here in this desolate place?" And he asked them, "How many loaves do you have?" They said, "Seven."

MARK 8:4–5 ESV

Dear Father, why do I ever worry about not having enough when I have You? You can create plenty from nothing. You fed thousands with seven loaves and a few fish. Surely You will take care of me. You command all, and Your power is limitless. You will supply everything I require, and I don't need to worry about a thing. I am Your child. *Of course* You will take care of me because You are a good, good Father. You are generous and kind. I'm sorry for doubting You and for letting worry and fear dominate my thoughts. I trust You. I know I will have enough. I know I'll have plenty to share. Thank You for the peace that comes from trusting You completely.

True Success

"What good is it for someone to gain the whole world, yet forfeit their soul?"
MARK 8:36 NIV

Dear Father, I worry too much about being successful. I want people to think well of me. I want them to be impressed. I also want to feel proud and hold my head high when I'm around other successful people. But when I focus too much on worldly success, I take my eyes off You. I know that success by the world's standards can steal my soul, my years, my relationships, and my life. Help me look for success by Your standards, Father. Remind me that true peace is found only in You, not in more money, a bigger house, a newer car, or whatever it is I think will bring me happiness. I want to live a soul-healthy, spirit-healthy life. Help me keep my eyes on You, Father. I want to live for You alone.

Childlike

People were bringing little children to Jesus for him to place his hands on them, but the disciples rebuked them. When Jesus saw this, he was indignant. He said to them, "Let the little children come to me, and do not hinder them, for the kingdom of God belongs to such as these. Truly I tell you, anyone who will not receive the kingdom of God like a little child will never enter it."

MARK 10:13–15 NIV

Dear Father, this passage presents a truth that's hard for adults to understand. You want us to be mature, yet You want us to be like little children? How can we be both? Yet the more I think about it, the more it makes sense. A small child is totally dependent on her parents for everything. She trusts them completely for all her care. She knows that she's loved and that they will meet all her needs. Give me that kind of trust, Father. Thank You for loving me and caring for all my needs.

Give Me Faith

"What do you want me to do for you?" Jesus asked him. The blind man said, "Rabbi, I want to see." "Go," said Jesus, "your faith has healed you." Immediately he received his sight and followed Jesus along the road.
MARK 10:51–52 NIV

. . . .

Dear Father, time and again in scripture, You commend faith. If I believe You will do it, You reward that kind of trust. Too often, there's a discrepancy between what I *say* I believe and what I *show* I believe. I say I have faith that You'll take care of me, but my actions don't support that. I worry and fret at the first sign of trouble, and my anxiety kicks into overdrive. I'm so sorry for my lack of consistency. I want to have the faith of this blind man, Father. I really do. Just as Jesus healed him of his blindness, please heal me of my unbelief.

The Colt

As they approached Jerusalem and came to Bethphage and Bethany at the Mount of Olives, Jesus sent two of his disciples, saying to them, "Go to the village ahead of you, and just as you enter it, you will find a colt tied there, which no one has ever ridden. Untie it and bring it here."

MARK 11:1–2 NIV

Dear Father, why would Jesus ask for a colt that had never been ridden? Normally, a colt needs to be trained. It would initially have trouble with a rider. It would certainly be skittish around a large crowd of people, many of them waving palm branches, as was the case in this passage. But this colt didn't need to be trained, because animals obey their masters. You created the colt, and Jesus is Your Son. Father, make me obedient like that colt. Sometimes, You ask me to do things I don't feel prepared for. Help me calm down and simply obey my Master.

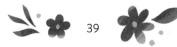

Teach Me to Forgive

"Therefore I tell you, whatever you ask in prayer, believe that you have received it, and it will be yours. And whenever you stand praying, forgive, if you have anything against anyone, so that your Father also who is in heaven may forgive you your trespasses."
MARK 11:24–25 ESV

Dear Father, when I read these verses, my worried attitude doesn't make sense. You've given me a direct line to Your presence, and You long to give me everything I need. The second part of this passage stings a little, though. You've forgiven me for so much, and You want me to show the same grace to others. If I don't feel like my prayers are being answered or even heard, I might want to check my heart. When I hold others' faults and failures against them, I also put up a wall between myself and You. Teach me to forgive, Father.

Embarrassed and Ashamed

"But go, tell his disciples and Peter that
he is going before you to Galilee. There
you will see him, just as he told you."
MARK 16:7 ESV

. . . .

Dear Father, at this pivotal moment, Peter was off by himself. He had separated from the group. He was ashamed because he'd promised to stand by Jesus until the end, and he didn't. Instead, three different times he denied even knowing Jesus! He was probably worried about what the others thought of him. I do the same thing. I worry about others' opinions of me. I'm afraid they're looking at my failures and judging me. But I know I can find peace in You. You don't judge me harshly. You are quick to forgive. Many times, others aren't judging me either. They're just trying to get through their own difficulties. Teach me not to withdraw from those I love when I feel embarrassed or ashamed. Thank You for Your grace.

The God of Second Chances

When he rose early on the first day of the
week, he appeared first to Mary Magdalene,
from whom he had cast out seven demons.
MARK 16:9 ESV

Dear Father, seven demons? Now *here* is a woman with a past. Yet You chose her to be the first one Christ appeared to after His resurrection. Sometimes I worry I'm not good enough. I worry what people think about me or what they'll say if they find out about all the skeletons in my closet. But You are the God of new beginnings and fresh starts. You reach down, grab hold of us, lift us out of the trash heap, and clean us off. Then You clothe us in Your righteousness and set us in a place of honor as Your child. Thank You for loving me despite my past. Thank You for being the God of second chances.

Don't Go Backward

Zechariah said to the angel, "How shall I know this?
For I am an old man, and my wife is advanced in
years." And the angel answered him, "I am Gabriel.
I stand in the presence of God, and I was sent to speak
to you and to bring you this good news. And behold,
you will be silent and unable to speak until the day
that these things take place, because you did not
believe my words, which will be fulfilled in their time."
Luke 1:18–20 esv

Dear Father, Zechariah was a priest. He was an *old* priest. He had served You faithfully for many years. He should have responded in faith, not doubt. Because he showed such a lack of faith, he was struck mute for several months. When I'm at a place in my life where I *should* trust You but I *don't*, there are consequences. Am I mature in my faith? I don't want to go backward and start doubting You. You have never ever failed me.

Absolutely Nothing

"For nothing will be impossible with God."
LUKE 1:37 ESV

Dear Father, this sentence is short and to the point. The angel explained to Mary that with You the rules of logic don't apply. You are almighty and all-powerful. Mary knew she couldn't conceive a child without having been with a man, but *nothing is impossible with You*. I know logic and reason are important tools for life. But they don't trump You! Often, You act within the confines of human understanding. But sometimes, You work miracles. You know the miracles I need in my life, Father. I trust You with all of it. I trust You with my children, my marriage, and my relationships. I trust You with my job and my finances. I trust You with all the things that steal my sleep. I place all of it in Your hands. I know nothing is impossible with You.

Mary's Song

"My soul magnifies the Lord, and my spirit rejoices in God my Savior, for he has looked on the humble estate of his servant. For behold, from now on all generations will call me blessed; for he who is mighty has done great things for me, and holy is his name. And his mercy is for those who fear him from generation to generation."

LUKE 1:46–50 ESV

. . . .

Dear Father, this passage is part of the song Mary sang to You when she realized she was carrying Your Son. But it could be my song too. You are mighty. You've done great things for me. You've taken care of me and seen me through wretched storms. You've never left me for a single moment. You are holy, and I love You. I'm so grateful for Your mercy, Father. You've poured out Your love on me, though I don't deserve it. Please be with the people I love, and spill out Your kindness on them for generations to come.

Peace

"Glory to God in the highest, and on earth peace among those with whom he is pleased!"
LUKE 2:14 ESV

. . . .

Dear Father, I love this verse. It's one of my favorite passages to read at Christmastime, written on the front of a greeting card with pictures of angels and shepherds. But the end of the verse often gets left off. You didn't send Your peace to everyone. You sent it to those You're pleased with. When we do our best to honor and obey You, when we talk to You daily and follow Your ways, You are pleased. When we act in humility and show kindness and grace to others, You are pleased. And when You are pleased, You shower us with peace even amid hardship. I want to please You, Father. Show me what I need to do to make You happy. Thank You for loving me and giving me peace.

No Room for Fear

But Mary treasured up all these things,
pondering them in her heart. And the shepherds
returned, glorifying and praising God for all they
had heard and seen, as it had been told them.

LUKE 2:19–20 ESV

Dear Father, Mary treasured all the things You did for her and pondered them in her heart. Each day, You do amazing things for me as well. Do I treasure them? Do I ponder them? Thinking about Your goodness brings gratitude and peace. When I fill my mind with Your love, kindness, and generosity, worry gets pushed out. Do I glorify and praise You like the shepherds? Do I tell others about all the great things You've done for me? I probably don't do that as much as I should. Change my thought patterns, Lord. Fill my mind with so much praise and gratitude that there's no room for fear.

Anna

And there was a prophetess, Anna, the daughter of Phanuel, of the tribe of Asher. She was advanced in years, having lived with her husband seven years from when she was a virgin, and then as a widow until she was eighty-four. She did not depart from the temple, worshiping with fasting and prayer night and day. And coming up at that very hour she began to give thanks to God and to speak of him to all who were waiting for the redemption of Jerusalem.

LUKE 2:36–38 ESV

Dear Father, Anna was a prophetess. At a time in history when women weren't well regarded, You placed her in an esteemed role. She had a hard life. But she didn't worry about how she'd provide for herself. Instead, she stayed close to the temple, where she knew she could serve You best. You honored her faithful life by letting her be among the first to announce Your Son's arrival. I want to be faithful too. And like Anna, I've already been blessed beyond measure.

Strong and Wise

And the child grew and became strong, filled with wisdom. And the favor of God was upon him.
LUKE 2:40 ESV

. . . .

Dear Father, what a beautiful thing to say about a child—Your child, Jesus. He was strong and wise. I want the same to be said about my children and the children I know and love. Instead of worrying about their future, I will pray for them. Instead of worrying over what will come, I commit to teach them Your ways. Make them strong and healthy, Lord. Make them kind and compassionate and loving. Give them the wisdom that only comes from You. Cast Your favor on them. Make them kind and successful and well liked. And show me what I can do to teach them and influence them in Your ways. Thank You for Jesus, and thank You for the beautiful children in my life.

Make Me Like You

*And Jesus increased in wisdom and in
stature and in favor with God and man.*
LUKE 2:52 ESV

Dear Father, reputation is important, isn't it? Sometimes I worry too much about what others think of me. I lose sleep if I think someone doesn't like me, and it drains my energy. I've been guilty of trying too hard to please people, to the point of exhaustion. But when I look at this verse, I'm reminded that as I grow in Your favor, I'll also grow in others' esteem. The qualities of a godly person are the characteristics that draw people to us. Instead of caring so much about what others think of me, I want You to make me more like You. Make me wise and kind and loving. Make me gentle and gracious and compassionate. The more I reflect Your character, the more I'll find favor with the people around me.

The Liar

And the devil took him up and showed him
all the kingdoms of the world in a moment
of time, and said to him, "To you I will give all
this authority and their glory, for it has been
delivered to me, and I give it to whom I will. If
you, then, will worship me, it will all be yours."

LUKE 4:5–7 ESV

Dear Father, Satan is a liar. If Jesus had worshipped him, Satan would not have delivered on his promise anyway or he would have taken it back. Satan lies to me all the time. He promises me things, and then he doesn't deliver. He tells me I'm not good enough. He tells me that terrible things are in store for my life. I know better than to believe him, even for a second, but he catches me off guard. Give me wisdom to recognize Satan's lies and the strength to put him in his place.

A Quiet Place

But now even more the report about him went abroad, and great crowds gathered to hear him and to be healed of their infirmities. But he would withdraw to desolate places and pray.
LUKE 5:15–16 ESV

Dear Father, Jesus needed space. He needed time away from the crowd. There is restoration in solitude. When the world crowds in and thoughts crowd my mind, it's easy to become anxious. Sometimes I just sit in that anxiety, trying to fix things, trying to work things out in my mind. But the more I try to manipulate a situation, the more anxious I become. When I'm drowning in worry and fear, remind me to find a quiet place. Remind me to simply rest in You. Remind me to pray, to think about Your goodness, and to sit in Your grace. Remind me to sink into Your presence, for that's where I'll find peace.

Your Power in Me

And all the crowd sought to touch him, for power came out from him and healed them all.

LUKE 6:19 ESV

. . . .

Dear Father, when I read Luke 6:19, I am awed to realize that Your power *physically* came out from Jesus. People knew that with just one touch they'd be healed. In many places in Your Word, You tell us we have the same power living in us. That makes sense because You live in Your children. Your power is activated through faith. With faith, we can move mountains! Thank You for Your strength, Your control, and Your might that live in me. Give me faith, and let that power switch be flipped on in my life. When I'm tempted to worry, remind me of who I am and whose I am. Teach me to take full advantage of Your muscle against any circumstance. Thank You for making me Your child and for giving me such a great inheritance.

Healer

*In that hour he healed many people of
diseases and plagues and evil spirits, and on
many who were blind he bestowed sight.*

LUKE 7:21 ESV

Dear Father, You are the Healer. You are the same yesterday, today, and tomorrow. Just as You healed people of diseases and plagues and evil spirits, I know You can heal me of despair, anxiety, and fear. I know You can heal my finances and my relationships. I know You can heal my spouse and my children and everyone I love, no matter what ails them and holds them back. I know You can heal our nation. I know You can do all these things, and I believe You will. Give me faith, Father, and heal us. Thank You for the peace that comes from knowing everything is under Your control. I love You, I trust You, and I know You are good.

Give Me Peace

And he said to the woman, "Your faith
has saved you; go in peace."
LUKE 7:50 ESV

. . . .

Dear Father, this is one of my favorite verses in all scripture. It's so simple in its message: faith and peace go hand in hand. The more faith I have, the more peace I have. When I trust You, I feel a serenity that can't be explained and can only be understood by those who truly know You. Today, Father, I want to ask for more faith because I need Your peace. When I worry, give me faith. When I'm anxious, give me faith. When I'm afraid of all kinds of things, give me faith in Your goodness, Your mercy, and Your love. Whisper reminders to cling to Your power and grace. Like the woman in this passage, I want to have faith so I can go in peace.

Only Believe

While he was still speaking, someone from the ruler's house came and said, "Your daughter is dead; do not trouble the Teacher any more." But Jesus on hearing this answered him, "Do not fear; only believe, and she will be well."

LUKE 8:49–50 ESV

Dear Father, this passage tells such a beautiful story of Jesus' compassion and grace. In my mind, I can hear Him speaking to the man: *"Do not fear; only believe."* When I sink into worry, I like to picture You speaking those words to me: *"Do not fear; only believe."* I worry about so many things, Father. But I know worry isn't something one of Your children should do. Help me view each trial and hardship as an opportunity for You to show off. It's a chance for You to demonstrate Your power and to work miracles in my life. Today, I choose not to fear. I will only believe.

Trust Me

And he said to them, "Take nothing for your
journey, no staff, nor bag, nor bread, nor money;
and do not have two tunics. And whatever house
you enter, stay there, and from there depart."
LUKE 9:3–4 ESV

Dear Father, in this passage, Jesus had called His twelve disciples together. He gave them the power and authority to cast out demons and cure diseases. Then He sent them out to tell everyone about God's love and heal the people of their hurts. Almost as an afterthought He said, "Oh, and when you go, don't take anything with you. It will just weigh you down. It will just be something you have to keep up with. As long as you're doing My will, I'll provide everything you need. Trust Me." You're still sending out Your disciples, and that includes me. And You still say to us, "Don't worry about *stuff*. I'll take care of everything you need. Trust Me."

Who Is He?

Then he said to them, "But who do you say that I am?" And Peter answered, "The Christ of God."
LUKE 9:20 ESV

Dear Father, if Christ is who I say He is, why do I worry about anything? Why this anxiety? With Christ on my side as my Brother, my Savior, and my God, what is the worst that could happen to me? Even if I die, I'll be with You in heaven. But still I worry. For me, I think the worst thing is humiliation. I worry too much about what others think. If I would just humble myself and kill my pride, so much of my worry would vanish. Clear out my thoughts, Father, and help me focus only on Your Son, Jesus. He is good and kind, and He loves me. He is all-powerful and will take care of every need. Thank You for Jesus.

Mary or Martha?

But the Lord answered her, "Martha, Martha, you are anxious and troubled about many things, but one thing is necessary. Mary has chosen the good portion, which will not be taken away from her."
LUKE 10:41–42 ESV

. . . .

Dear Father, I've often wondered if I'm a Mary or a Martha. The truth is I'm both. Sometimes I'm a Mary, laying aside all my worries, sitting at Your feet, and worshipping. Other times I'm a Martha, hustling and hauling to get things done. When I'm distracted, anxious, or troubled, my response is often busyness. I try to control things with my actions. But the best response is always the *Mary* response. When worry drives me to frantic busyness, remind me to calm down and just sit at Your feet. . .to hear Your words. . .to rest in You. I want to soak in Your presence, Lord, and be filled with Your peace.

When You Don't Know What to Say

*"Now when they bring you before the synagogues
and the officials and the authorities, do not worry
about how or what you are to speak in your defense,
or what you are to say; for the Holy Spirit will teach
you in that very hour what you ought to say."*
LUKE 12:11–12 NASB

Dear Father, this has happened to me so many times. I find myself in an unexpected or tricky situation, and I don't know what to say. I often just ramble on without thinking through my thoughts, and my words land me in more trouble. But when I enter a situation with a spirit of prayer, Your Holy Spirit gives me the right words to say—words I hadn't planned and couldn't come up with on my own. Next time I find myself at a loss for words, remind me not to panic. I just need to pause, pray, and trust You with the outcome.

Remind Me

And Herod, together with his soldiers, treated Him with contempt and mocked Him, dressing Him in a brightly shining robe, and sent Him back to Pilate.

Luke 23:11 NASB

Dear Father, I don't know if there's anything more humiliating than being mocked. Jesus had done nothing but good. He loved people, healed them, and pointed them to You, yet He was mocked. But Jesus didn't respond with anger or vengeance. He maintained His dignity and let them hurl their insults. He kept loving them despite their cruelty. Remind me of this the next time I feel that others are mocking me without cause. When others laugh at me or gossip about me, pull me close to You. Remind me that You see. You know. And You remember. Help me keep shining Your light. Help me keep loving those around me, even when they're unkind.

When Life Is Unfair

*And when they led Him away, they seized
a man, Simon of Cyrene, as he was coming
in from the country, and placed on him
the cross to carry behind Jesus.*

LUKE 23:26 NASB

Dear Father, Simon of Cyrene was an innocent bystander. He'd done nothing to deserve this treatment. He just happened to be in the wrong place at the wrong time. Sometimes we're called to do things that aren't fair. They don't make sense, and we wonder why they're happening. At the time, Simon had no way of knowing this event would give him a place of honor in the greatest story ever told. In the same way, my unfair hardship may be designed to catapult me to honor and blessing I couldn't have imagined. Help me accept whatever comes my way, knowing You're in control and You love me beyond measure.

Disregarded

*Now these women were Mary Magdalene, Joanna,
and Mary the mother of James; also the other
women with them were telling these things to
the apostles. But these words appeared to them as
nonsense, and they would not believe the women.*

Luke 24:10–11 NASB

. . . .

Dear Father, at Jesus' time in history, women were treated with little regard. The women in this passage spoke the truth, but their words were considered nonsense. Sometimes I feel disregarded as well. I feel that I have important things to say and valuable experience to add, but others treat me like I don't matter. That hurts, Father. When that happens, remind me of this story. You chose the humble, the lowly, the disregarded people of the world to be important messengers of Your truth. You don't underestimate Your daughters; You don't underestimate me. Help me live up to Your expectations and disregard any opinion that doesn't line up with Your Word.

Power

In the beginning was the Word, and the Word was with God, and the Word was God. He was in the beginning with God. All things came into being through Him, and apart from Him not even one thing came into being that has come into being. In Him was life, and the life was the Light of mankind. And the Light shines in the darkness, and the darkness did not grasp it.

JOHN 1:1–5 NASB

Dear Father, each time I read this passage, I feel jolts of electricity run through me. Your words are power because You are the Word! *Christ* is the Word. When I speak Your Word, I speak Christ into a situation. When I speak Your Word, I inject all Your muscle into that experience. Your words aren't a bunch of antiquated, dusty ideas. They are living and active and sharper than any two-edged sword. They are full of life and strength and love. I want to hide Your words in my heart. Bring them to my lips every day.

The Good Stuff

*Now when the headwaiter tasted the water which
had become wine, and did not know where it came
from (but the servants who had drawn the water
knew), the headwaiter called the groom, and said
to him, "Every man serves the good wine first, and
when the guests are drunk, then he serves the poorer
wine; but you have kept the good wine until now."*

JOHN 2:9–10 NASB

Dear Father, I love this story. It's a great reminder that You can make something special out of nothing special. Often this "good wine" comes from a bad situation, just as it did in the story. The good stuff can be surprising. Father, please take the water of my life and turn it into something far better than I could have imagined. I need a miracle, and You're the only One who can deliver it. I trust You completely. I wait with expectation, knowing You have good things in store.

Power to Bend

Then, when they had rowed about twenty-five or thirty stadia, they saw Jesus walking on the sea and coming near the boat; and they were frightened. But He said to them, "It is I; do not be afraid." So they were willing to take Him into the boat, and immediately the boat was at the land to which they were going.

JOHN 6:19–21 NASB

Dear Father, Christ bent the laws of physics. He bent the laws of time. Why do I forget Your power? Why do I worry about anything? I know even the most unlikely result can come about with a word from Your lips, a touch of Your hand. Father, You know the needs of my heart. You see the storms raging around me. Right now, I feel like I'll drown. Speak a miracle into being, Lord. Calm my fears. I trust You to bend circumstances and control time. I know You love me, and I trust Your kindness and love.

Let the River Flow

Now on the last day, the great day of the feast,
Jesus stood and cried out, saying, "If anyone
is thirsty, let him come to Me and drink. The one
who believes in Me, as the Scripture said, 'From his
innermost being will flow rivers of living water.'"
JOHN 7:37–38 NASB

Dear Father, it feels like Jesus is speaking these words directly to me. I am thirsty, Lord. I'm parched. I long for Your living water. You know the circumstances of my life that cause me to worry. Fear sucks the life out of me. It drains my energy until I have nothing left to give. I feel withered and dried up. But I believe in You, Father! I believe in Your Son. Pour those living springs into my spirit. Flow through my veins. Fill the air I breathe with Your presence. I'm thirsty. Satiate me with Your love.

Whom to Listen To

"You are of your father the devil, and you want to do the desires of your father. He was a murderer from the beginning, and does not stand in the truth because there is no truth in him. Whenever he tells a lie, he speaks from his own nature, because he is a liar and the father of lies. But because I say the truth, you do not believe Me."

JOHN 8:44–45 NASB

Dear Father, I know I'm prone to believe Satan's lies because they are familiar and comfortable. He's been whispering those lies into my spirit since I was born. It's harder to believe Your truth because it's not as familiar. Yet I know, deep down, that Satan is a liar. He wants to destroy me. You are my loving Father, and Your words have life. When those negative voices fill my mind with lies, help me call them out and send them away. You love me, and You speak truth. I will listen to You.

Hide Me

Jesus said to them, "Truly, truly I say to you, before Abraham was born, I am." Therefore they picked up stones to throw at Him, but Jesus hid Himself and left the temple grounds.
JOHN 8:58–59 NASB

Dear Father, I don't know why more attention isn't given to this little story. Jesus hid Himself! Scripture doesn't really go into detail. We don't know how He did it. But when trouble came and they wanted to kill Him before it was time, He disappeared. He became invisible to them, and He escaped. Jesus, just as You hid Yourself from trouble, will You hide me? Hide me in the shadow of Your wings. Hide me in the palm of Your hands. Hide me from trouble and despair, from financial ruin and disease, from relationship troubles, fear, and anxiety. Only let Your goodness and love find me. Surround me with Your peace. I love You and trust You.

Remain

"Remain in Me, and I in you. Just as the branch cannot bear fruit of itself but must remain in the vine, so neither can you unless you remain in Me. I am the vine, you are the branches; the one who remains in Me, and I in him bears much fruit, for apart from Me you can do nothing."
JOHN 15:4–5 NASB

. . . .

Dear Father, to remain means to stay. If a branch is severed from the vine, it dies. It certainly won't produce any fruit if it's not attached. But a branch attached to a healthy vine will produce fruit without even trying. The fruit is a natural by-product of remaining attached to the vine. Father, when I lack peace in my life, I guess I need to make sure I'm remaining in You. When I choose worry and fear over trusting You, I'm really choosing to sever my connection to You. Help me remain in You, and please fill the branches of my life with Your peace.

Put Away Your Sword

So Jesus said to Peter, "Put the sword into the sheath; the cup which the Father has given Me, am I not to drink it?"
JOHN 18:11 NASB

. . . .

Dear Father, Peter and I have a lot in common. He wanted to fight against circumstances he didn't like instead of staying calm and letting You handle things. But everything that happened was a part of Your plan. Even in the worst circumstances, You have a purpose. I know all Your plans for me are good. Even if they don't feel great while I'm going through them, I know You will lead me to a place of peace, joy, and love. Forgive me for getting angsty and striking out against situations instead of just letting You fight my battles. Forgive me for taking out my sword when You want me to be still. I know every battle belongs to You, and in the end, I'll see victory.

Reaching through the Dark

But when the day was now breaking,
Jesus stood on the beach; yet the disciples
did not know that it was Jesus.

JOHN 21:4 NASB

. . . .

Dear Father, You don't always show up in obvious ways, do You? In this story, Jesus stood quietly on the beach. He didn't announce Himself or draw attention. When I get anxious, I want You to reveal Yourself with a trumpet blast or a flashing neon sign. But often, You show Yourself in the whisper. You make Yourself barely visible through the fog. You want me to reach my hand through the dark places and trust that You'll pull me out. You promised You will always reveal Yourself to those who earnestly seek You and whose hearts are tender toward You. I'm here, Lord. I trust Your love for me. Show Yourself. I'm reaching for You, Father. Please make Yourself known.

Claiming the Promise

"It is you who are the sons of the prophets and of the covenant which God ordained with your fathers, saying to Abraham, 'AND IN YOUR SEED ALL THE FAMILIES OF THE EARTH SHALL BE BLESSED.'"
ACTS 3:25 NASB

Dear Father, I know these words weren't spoken directly to me, but I'd like to claim them anyway. You said to Abraham that he and his offspring would be blessed. Today, I lift up the names of each member of my family and ask You to bless them. I ask You to place Your hand on them. Draw them close to You. Put the stamp of Your Holy Spirit on them and make them Yours. Pull them into Your presence and keep them safe. Let each of them be a vessel of Your kindness, a mirror of Your goodness, and a channel of Your love. May each of them honor You with their lives. Count my family as part of Your blessing, Lord.

About Regret

*Now Saul approved of putting Stephen to death.
And on that day a great persecution began
against the church in Jerusalem, and they were
all scattered throughout the regions of Judea
and Samaria, except for the apostles.*

ACTS 8:1 NASB

Dear Father, Saul approved of the stoning of Stephen, the first martyr. Talk about regret! Saul later became the apostle Paul, and he had to live with the fact that he'd caused the death of other Christ followers. But regret isn't always a bad thing. It's bad if it paralyzes us. But for Saul, that regret fueled his determination to change, to somehow make things right, and to carry on Your work. We can see now that the scattering mentioned here actually brought the gospel to more people. Satan intended this for harm, but You intended it for good. Help me view the bad circumstances of my life in light of eternity. What can I learn? How can I change? How can this help to spread Your love to the world around me?

When We Disagree

Now it turned into such a sharp disagreement that they separated from one another, and Barnabas took Mark with him and sailed away to Cyprus. But Paul chose Silas, and left after being entrusted by the brothers to the grace of the Lord. And he was traveling through Syria and Cilicia, strengthening the churches.
ACTS 15:39–41 NASB

Dear Father, relationships can be difficult. You made us all unique. You created us with different gifts, talents, experiences, and thought patterns. These differences can lead to disagreements, which can lead to hurt feelings and separation. I know You want me to live at peace with others as much as possible. But the feud between Barnabas and Paul wasn't over doctrinal issues or spiritual things. It was a simple disagreement, and when they couldn't come to a resolution, they decided to part ways. This split actually caused a speedier and more thorough spread of the gospel. Help me honor You in all my relationships, and help me view personal disagreements in light of eternity.

Not My Own

"But I do not consider my life of any account as dear to myself, so that I may finish my course and the ministry which I received from the Lord Jesus, to testify solemnly of the gospel of God's grace."
ACTS 20:24 NASB

Dear Father, my life is not my own. It is Yours to do with as You want. My comfort and rest will come when my work on earth is done. Any comfort and rest I experience here is just an added bonus to what You already have planned for me in eternity. Pleasure is not my purpose. All these statements are hard for me to commit to, and saying them now breaks me a little bit inside. I've been through some hard things in my life, and I don't understand why it has to hurt so much. Yet here I am, Father. I'm Yours. Do with me as You please.

God's Plans

But the son of Paul's sister heard about their ambush, and he came and entered the barracks and told Paul. Paul called one of the centurions to himself and said, "Take this young man to the commander, for he has something to report to him."
ACTS 23:16–17 NASB

Dear Father, if Paul's time had been up, he'd have been killed. But instead when men plotted in secret to kill Paul, You placed Paul's nephew there to intervene. I know Your plan will not be thwarted in my life either. If I'm supposed to have a certain job or relationship, I will. If I'm supposed to do something for You, You will clear the path and make it happen. Even when it feels like the world is against me, I know I can rest in You. As long as I stay close to You and try to please You, Your purpose for my life will be fulfilled. I know Your plans for me are good, and I trust You completely.

Out of My Control

Now when it was decided that we would sail for Italy, they proceeded to turn Paul and some other prisoners over to a centurion of the Augustan cohort, named Julius. And we boarded an Adramyttian ship that was about to sail to the regions along the coast of Asia, and put out to sea accompanied by Aristarchus, a Macedonian of Thessalonica.

Acts 27:1–2 NASB

Dear Father, Paul didn't get to make the decision about whether he'd go to Italy. That choice was made for him. In the same way, I don't always get to decide about certain things in my life. I don't get to control how things turn out. You're the One who decides. I can be submissive or rebellious to Your plans. I've learned things are a lot easier for me when I submit to Your will and purpose for my life. I'm Yours, Lord. Do with me as You will. I trust You.

About Retirement

Now Paul stayed two full years in his own rented lodging and welcomed all who came to him, preaching the kingdom of God and teaching things about the Lord Jesus Christ with all openness, unhindered.
ACTS 28:30–31 NASB

. . . .

Dear Father, were there retirement plans in Paul's day? I don't think so. Paul worked until he was no longer able to work. He fulfilled Your purpose for his life, and he paid his own way through it. Like Paul, I know You want me to work for You until I'm no longer able. . .and as long as I have breath, I'll be able to work—whether through physical labor or prayer. Paul didn't set aside the last decades of his life for leisure. You've set aside eternity for my rest. Remind me not to worry about retirement, Father. Help me invest wisely, knowing that ultimately You'll take care of all my needs until my time here is complete.

From Faith for Faith

For I am not ashamed of the gospel, for it is the power of God for salvation to everyone who believes, to the Jew first and also to the Greek. For in it the righteousness of God is revealed from faith for faith, as it is written, "The righteous shall live by faith."
ROMANS 1:16–17 ESV

Dear Father, You keep putting me in situations where faith is required, don't You? Paul wrote that Your righteousness is revealed "from faith for faith." That's an interesting way to word that concept. I wonder if he meant that the act of faith actually produces more faith. The more I trust You with hard things, the easier it is to trust You in the future. By placing me in circumstances where faith is needed, You are actually giving me a chance to grow stronger. I trust You, Father. Give me faith!

In Hope

In hope he believed against hope, that he should become the father of many nations, as he had been told, "So shall your offspring be." He did not weaken in faith when he considered his own body, which was as good as dead (since he was about a hundred years old), or when he considered the barrenness of Sarah's womb. No unbelief made him waver concerning the promise of God, but he grew strong in his faith as he gave glory to God.
ROMANS 4:18–20 ESV

Dear Father, in hope Abraham believed. Hope is the opposite of worry, fear, and anxiety. Hope believes for good things, but worry believes for something negative. Make me like Abraham, Father. Right now, my default button is set to fear. Reset it to hope. I want to free-fall into Your goodness and grace. Help me exhale the toxic fumes of anxiety and breathe in Your life-giving love. Build my faith, for I know that faith will lead to the beautiful peace only You can give.

Set Free

*For if we have been united with him in a death like his,
we shall certainly be united with him in a resurrection
like his. We know that our old self was crucified with
him in order that the body of sin might be brought to
nothing, so that we would no longer be enslaved to
sin. For one who has died has been set free from sin.*
ROMANS 6:5–7 ESV

Dear Father, worry is sin. It shows a lack of faith in Your goodness and love. It's hard to break free of that thought pattern, Lord. It's become a familiar way of life for me. But I'm no longer enslaved to old, sinful patterns. They don't control me anymore—You do! Because of what Christ did for me on the cross, I've been set free. I don't have to succumb to Satan's lies. I don't have to kowtow to fear and anxiety. I am wrapped in Your grace and floating in Your love. Thank You for setting me free!

New Life

For while we were living in the flesh, our sinful passions, aroused by the law, were at work in our members to bear fruit for death. But now we are released from the law, having died to that which held us captive, so that we serve in the new way of the Spirit and not in the old way of the written code.

ROMANS 7:5–6 ESV

Dear Father, Christ bore the brunt of my sin when He died on the cross. But in a way, I died with Him. My sins died. My shame died. Everything that keeps me enslaved and burdened died. Anxiety doesn't rule me any longer! When I give time and attention to worry and fear, it's like forcing life into something putrid and dead. . .like inviting a zombie to take over my thoughts. Thank You for nailing all my sins to the cross. Help me leave them there as I embrace my new life in You.

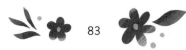

Little Sister

For those whom he foreknew he also predestined to be conformed to the image of his Son, in order that he might be the firstborn among many brothers. And those whom he predestined he also called, and those whom he called he also justified, and those whom he justified he also glorified.
ROMANS 8:29–30 ESV

Dear Father, when You say Christ is the firstborn among many brothers, You're talking about me, aren't You? Christ is the firstborn, but I'm also in the family. Christ is my older Brother because I'm Your child too. I'm the little sister. I'm "in." I'm an heir to Your riches, just as Christ is. I can't imagine why You love me so much, but I'm so grateful that You do. When I'm tempted to focus on this world's temporary troubles, pull me back. Remind me who I am and whose I am. I'm so proud to say I belong to You.

84

Mosaic

For the Scripture says to Pharaoh, "For this very purpose I have raised you up, that I might show my power in you, and that my name might be proclaimed in all the earth."

ROMANS 9:17 ESV

Dear Father, all things happen with Your permission. There is nothing my mind can concoct to worry about that isn't already under Your control. I can worry about politics, but You've got that covered. No one is in power without Your nod, and You will cause even the most vile government official to help bring about Your purpose. I can worry about money or health or relationships, but those too are under Your control. You don't cause evil, but You allow bad things to happen so You can show Your power in the world. Thank You for taking the most shattered situations, scooping up the pieces, and using them to create a beautiful mosaic of Your love.

How to Grow My Faith

So faith comes from hearing, and
hearing through the word of Christ.
ROMANS 10:17 ESV

Dear Father, when I worry about things, I waste my time. I'm choosing to spend the precious moments of my life on something fruitless and vain. But when I read Your Word, I insert power into my life. Your Word infuses every situation with Your strength and authority. And when I take it a step further and actually do the things You tell me to do, my faith grows even more. The power gets even stronger. Forgive me for spending time in futile worry. When I'm tempted to go there in my mind, pull me to Your Word. Show me productive things I can do, like praying, praising You, and serving others. Grow my faith, Father. I want a strong faith, which comes from knowing and claiming Your promises.

His Endless Wisdom

Oh, the depth of the riches and wisdom and knowledge of God! How unsearchable are his judgments and how inscrutable his ways!
ROMANS 11:33 ESV

. . . .

Dear Father, Your ways are so far above my understanding. When I get bogged down in worry, I'm really choosing to wallow in my limited level of comprehension instead of having faith in Your wisdom. Forgive me for trying to figure things out on my own. Things are hopeless if left to me. That's why I sink into fear and anxiety. But I can choose to operate on a higher plane—a faith plane. Thank You for Your endless wisdom and kindness and grace. It doesn't matter if I can figure things out on my own. I trust You completely, and I know You have everything all worked out according to Your grace.

Instead of Worry

*Let love be genuine. Abhor what is evil; hold
fast to what is good. Love one another with
brotherly affection. Outdo one another in showing
honor. Do not be slothful in zeal, be fervent in spirit,
serve the Lord. Rejoice in hope, be patient in
tribulation, be constant in prayer. Contribute to the
needs of the saints and seek to show hospitality.*
Romans 12:9–13 esv

Dear Father, I've heard that if we don't have enough to do, Satan will find something to fill our time. This is true in my own life. When I have too much time on my hands, my thoughts turn to worry. But this passage gives me a list of productive things I can do to stay busy and keep my mind from sin. I can look for ways to love people, to do good, to show honor and hospitality, and to help those in need. When I focus my attention inward, anxiety strikes. When I direct my energy toward others, Your peace follows.

Don't Feed the Worry

But put on the Lord Jesus Christ, and make no provision for the flesh, to gratify its desires.

ROMANS 13:14 ESV

. . . .

Dear Father, I am Your child, which means I'm now governed by Your Holy Spirit. I don't have to give in to every whim of my flesh like I did before I belonged to You. Anxiety and fear have no power over me. Though I can't control each thought that enters my mind, I can control which thoughts I invite to stay. My old sin nature still tries to boss me around, but I know I can dismiss it like a tiny barking Chihuahua. When I'm tempted to feed my worry, remind me that the more I nurture those thoughts, the more they'll make themselves at home in my life. Remind me who I am, and help me act with confidence and authority over my old sin nature.

Abound in Hope

*May the God of hope fill you with all joy and
peace in believing, so that by the power of
the Holy Spirit you may abound in hope.*
ROMANS 15:13 ESV

Dear Father, to abound means to be plentiful and abundant. It means to flourish and thrive. I love that You want me to *abound* in hope. You want me to flourish and thrive in the confidence that You have good and wonderful things in store for me. Satan wants the opposite. He's a liar, and every day he tries to convince me that terrible things are in store. But even when Satan hits me with his best shot, You sit back and say, "That's the best you can do, Satan? Watch this." Then You proceed to take even the worst circumstance and turn it into something beautiful and powerful and amazing. Thank You for Your hope, Father. When I'm tempted to worry, remind me to thrive in You.

No Lack

I give thanks to my God always for you because of the grace of God that was given you in Christ Jesus, that in every way you were enriched in him in all speech and all knowledge—even as the testimony about Christ was confirmed among you—so that you are not lacking in any gift, as you wait for the revealing of our Lord Jesus Christ.
1 CORINTHIANS 1:4–7 ESV

Dear Father, Satan tells me I'm not good enough. He attacks my self-confidence and drives me to worry. . .about what others think of me, about my failures, about how my lack will affect the people I love. But that's not what You say about me at all, is it? You say I'm not lacking in any gift. You've given me everything I need to live out the full purpose You planned for me before I was born. Thank You for this reminder that I'm wonderfully made and fully equipped to live my best life for You.

God's Choice

But God chose what is foolish in the world to shame the wise; God chose what is weak in the world to shame the strong; God chose what is low and despised in the world, even things that are not, to bring to nothing things that are, so that no human being might boast in the presence of God.

1 CORINTHIANS 1:27–29 ESV

Dear Father, according to these verses, I don't ever need to worry about not being good enough. To You, lack of intelligence or worldly wisdom is a plus. To You, lack of finances isn't a problem. To You, lack of political or social power is desirable. All these qualities, labeled as weakness by the world, are the same qualities that lead to humility. And to You, humility is a highly desired trait. Teach me to be humble, Father. Whenever I'm worrying over my lack, make me excited to see how You'll work through my weakness to show Your power.

Focus on Eternity

Do you not know that in a race all the runners run, but only one receives the prize? So run that you may obtain it. Every athlete exercises self-control in all things. They do it to receive a perishable wreath, but we an imperishable.

1 Corinthians 9:24–25 esv

Dear Father, help me keep my eye on the prize. I won't get the true prize this side of eternity, but that doesn't make the reward any less real. I know heaven isn't just a fantasy or a figment of my imagination. It's an actual place, and one day it will be more real to me than anything I experience here on earth. Unlike rewards I receive here, which are temporary, the prize I run for is eternal. Most of my worries are focused on temporary problems. Teach me to focus on eternity. I want to run this race called life in a way that pleases You. I'm running to win!

Praise Walk

But I say, walk by the Spirit, and you will not gratify the desires of the flesh. For the desires of the flesh are against the Spirit, and the desires of the Spirit are against the flesh, for these are opposed to each other, to keep you from doing the things you want to do. But if you are led by the Spirit, you are not under the law.

GALATIANS 5:16–18 ESV

Dear Father, walking is one of the best ways to get in shape physically. In a similar way, when I walk by Your Spirit, I become spiritually strong. When I walk by Your Spirit, I'm less likely to worry about things that are out of my control. I think the best way to walk with You is to praise You. Praise is my constant conversation with You. When I'm tempted to worry, remind me to get my walking shoes on and praise You!

Roots and Fruit

But the fruit of the Spirit is love, joy, peace, patience, kindness, goodness, faithfulness, gentleness, self-control; against such things there is no law.
GALATIANS 5:22–23 ESV

. . . .

Dear Father, I often focus on the fruit in my life instead of the roots. But if the roots aren't healthy, there won't be any fruit. Am I impatient? I need to walk with Your Spirit. Unkind? I need to spend more time with You. Your Spirit produces fruit. I can't produce it on my own. I know worry is not a fruit of Your Spirit. It's a fruit of the devil! When I spend time worrying, I'm really cultivating that bad fruit. That's not what I want. Remind me to spend quality time with You each day, talking to You in my mind, praising You, and learning from You. Help me develop quality roots so my life will produce bountiful fruit.

Adopted

He chose us in him before the foundation of the world, that we should be holy and blameless before him. In love he predestined us for adoption to himself as sons through Jesus Christ, according to the purpose of his will, to the praise of his glorious grace, with which he has blessed us in the Beloved.

EPHESIANS 1:4–6 ESV

Dear Father, I don't understand how You chose me. It goes beyond my comprehension. You could have chosen anyone You wanted. You certainly could have created a large biological family for Yourself. Instead, You chose the adoption route. You picked me out of a lineup and said, "That one. I want her. She belongs to Me. I'm making her My daughter, with full rights and inheritance as My own child." When Satan tries to tell me I'm not good enough, remind me that my value has nothing to do with who I am. It has everything to do with who my Father is.

Incomprehensible

*Now to him who is able to do far more abundantly
than all that we ask or think, according to
the power at work within us, to him be glory
in the church and in Christ Jesus throughout
all generations, forever and ever. Amen.*

EPHESIANS 3:20–21 ESV

Dear Father, when I read these verses, all I can think to say is "Wow!" You are amazing, Lord. Your ways are higher than mine; You are incomprehensible. Yet You can be known by someone like me. That blows my mind. Why do I forget so easily, so quickly? I don't need to worry about a thing. I belong to You, and You are all-powerful. I have access to the full treasure trove of Your riches, which includes peace and the assurance that You love me and will always work on my behalf. I'm so grateful to be Your daughter, Lord. Change my heart, and reprogram my mind to think like a child of the King.

Sword Practice

Finally, be strong in the Lord and in the strength of his might. Put on the whole armor of God, that you may be able to stand against the schemes of the devil.
EPHESIANS 6:10–11 ESV

Dear Father, Paul closed his letter to the Ephesians with this advice: Be strong in the Lord. Be ready to fight! With all that's going on in the world today, it's so important for me to be armed and ready for battle. This isn't a physical battle, fought with guns and jets. It's a spiritual battle, and You've already supplied me with top-of-the-line armor. You've given me the strongest weapon in existence: Your Word. Draw me into Your presence, Father, and help me spend time in Your Word. With each verse read, each section memorized, I sharpen my sword. Instead of worrying, I'll spend time in sword practice.

Ready for Battle

*For it has been granted to you that for the sake of
Christ you should not only believe in him but also
suffer for his sake, engaged in the same conflict
that you saw I had and now hear that I still have.*
PHILIPPIANS 1:29–30 ESV

. . . .

Dear Father, the idea that the Christian life is an easy one, free from suffering and persecution, is false. You want me to face life's battles with confidence, chin high and shoulders back. I am here to do Your bidding. Paul's suffering—his imprisonment for Christ's cause—resulted in much of the New Testament being written. What might my trials bring about? How might my difficulties make a mark for Your kingdom? When I face struggles, I'm often tempted to worry. That's exactly what Satan wants. He uses my fears to distract me. Make me a strong, wise warrior, Father. Remind me to push fear to the side and stand strong, ready to fight.

The Main Goals

*That I may know him and the power of
his resurrection, and may share his
sufferings, becoming like him in his death.*
PHILIPPIANS 3:10 ESV

Dear Father, thank You for this reminder of the important goals in my life. When I worry, I set those goals aside and focus on something less important. My main objectives are to know You, to experience Your power, and to be like You. To know You is not head knowledge but rather intimate heart knowledge. I want to know You more. If I claim to know You but don't experience Your power, something is wrong. The most obvious way to feel Your power is through conquering sin in my life, and that includes worry. And if I claim to be Your child but the people around me don't see the family resemblance, something is missing. Help me aim for these targets, Father. Everything else is just a distraction.

Nailed to the Cross

*And you, who were dead in your trespasses
and the uncircumcision of your flesh, God made
alive together with him, having forgiven us all
our trespasses, by canceling the record of debt
that stood against us with its legal demands.
This he set aside, nailing it to the cross.*

COLOSSIANS 2:13–14 ESV

Dear Father, most of the things I worry about have already been taken care of. That makes worry a waste of my time and energy. When I worry about my past, I can look to these verses. When I worry about whether I'm good enough, I can read this passage. When I hear Satan's lies and accusations, I can quote these words to him. You've forgiven all my sins. You've canceled all my spiritual debts. You've taken every failure and nailed it to the cross along with a note that says "Paid in full." Thank You for covering my debts.

Stay Focused

*Continue steadfastly in prayer, being
watchful in it with thanksgiving.*
COLOSSIANS 4:2 ESV

Dear Father, I am easily distracted. No matter how hard I try to focus on a goal, other things pull at my attention. Paul must have been familiar with distraction as he penned these words. He reminded the Colossians to stay focused on the important things.

Worry distracts me from my purpose. When I let worry into my thoughts, I forget my main goals in life: to be closer to You and to be more like You. When fears push in, remind me to stay focused. Remind me to keep praying. Remind me to be thankful. As I remain consistent in these tasks, worry will get crowded out by praise.

One Day

For the Lord himself will descend from heaven
with a cry of command, with the voice of an
archangel, and with the sound of the trumpet of
God. And the dead in Christ will rise first. Then
we who are alive, who are left, will be caught up
together with them in the clouds to meet the Lord
in the air, and so we will always be with the Lord.

1 Thessalonians 4:16–17 esv

. . . .

Dear Father, wow! I can't wait. When I read this passage, my heart speeds up, my blood pounds through my veins, and I almost lose my breath. What a day that will be! I'm so excited to finally meet You face-to-face. When I consider that day, it puts everything else into perspective. All my worries, fears, and failures will be just a shadow next to Your brightness. All my anxieties will fade away next to Your brilliance. When I succumb to fear, remind me that everything in this life will seem insignificant in light of eternity.

Simple Instructions

Rejoice always, pray without ceasing, give thanks in all circumstances; for this is the will of God in Christ Jesus for you.
1 Thessalonians 5:16–18 esv

Dear Father, thank You for these simple replacements for worry. No matter my concerns, they will fade away when I follow these short commands. They're not hard. I'm perfectly capable of doing these things. But for some reason, I forget. Do I rejoice always? No. I don't. Teach me to rejoice even in tough times. Because of You, I have a reason to rejoice. Do I pray without ceasing? Sometimes, but not always. When storms kick up in my life, I often resort to fear and worry. Remind me to turn to You first and not as a last resort. Do I give thanks in all circumstances? Not really. When life stinks, help me find things to be grateful for. No matter what, I'm always thankful for Your love.

When Others Hurt Me

Indeed God considers it just to repay with affliction those who afflict you, and to grant relief to you who are afflicted as well as to us, when the Lord Jesus is revealed from heaven with his mighty angels in flaming fire, inflicting vengeance on those who do not know God and on those who do not obey the gospel of our Lord Jesus.

2 THESSALONIANS 1:6–8 ESV

Dear Father, justice for all will happen when Jesus comes back. We are eternal beings, and those who reject Christ will ultimately pay for their sins. All their deeds will be accounted for. For those who accept Your Son, our sins were accounted for on the cross. When people hurt me or those I love, when people do all kinds of evil, remind me that vengeance and punishment belong to You. You see it all. You know. And You don't want me to worry about it. Help me let go of the hurt and trust You.

The Real Treasures

The love of money is a root of all kinds of evils. It is through this craving that some have wandered away from the faith and pierced themselves with many pangs. But as for you, O man of God, flee these things. Pursue righteousness, godliness, faith, love, steadfastness, gentleness. Fight the good fight of the faith. Take hold of the eternal life to which you were called and about which you made the good confession in the presence of many witnesses.
1 Timothy 6:10–12 esv

Dear Father, why do I worry about money? Money itself is not bad. But spending too much time and energy focused on money—on how to get more of it or how to spend it— causes me to take my focus off You. You've made it clear what You want me to pursue: righteousness, godliness, faith, love, steadfastness, and gentleness. These are the real riches. Help me trust You with my finances and focus my efforts on the true treasures of Your kingdom.

Fight the Good Fight

*I have fought the good fight, I have finished the race,
I have kept the faith. Henceforth there is laid up for
me the crown of righteousness, which the
Lord, the righteous judge, will award to me
on that day, and not only to me but also
to all who have loved his appearing.*

2 TIMOTHY 4:7–8 ESV

Dear Father, when worry controls my life, I'm not really fighting the good fight, am I? I'm not keeping the faith. Worry does nothing to make me stronger. It doesn't change circumstances or conquer fears. Instead, worry causes my fears to grow. It makes me feel defeated. It robs me of my joy and steals my sleep. When fear crowds in, remind me to put on my armor and fight. You created me to be a victor, not a victim. I know You fight alongside me, and with You on my side, I am more than a conqueror.

Like You

Therefore he had to be made like his brothers in every respect, so that he might become a merciful and faithful high priest in the service of God, to make propitiation for the sins of the people. For because he himself has suffered when tempted, he is able to help those who are being tempted.

<small>HEBREWS 2:17–18 ESV</small>

Dear Father, I don't know where I got the idea that the Christian life should be easy. Somewhere along the way, I adopted the belief that as long as I'm following Your rules and living the best way I can, I'll be exempt from suffering. When difficulties come my way, I worry and stress and wonder what I've done to deserve such a bad lot. But hardship makes me strong. Hardship makes me beautiful because it makes me more like You. It's through the storms of life that I become kinder, gentler, and more compassionate. I won't invite the hard things, Father. But when they come, use them to make me like You.

Watch Your Tongue!

If anyone thinks he is religious and does not bridle his tongue but deceives his heart, this person's religion is worthless. Religion that is pure and undefiled before God the Father is this: to visit orphans and widows in their affliction, and to keep oneself unstained from the world.

JAMES 1:26–27 ESV

Dear Father, I've usually thought about these verses as they relate to gossip, slander, and foul language. I need to control my tongue so it doesn't hurt anyone, right? That application is beneficial, but today, as I read this passage, worry comes to mind. How many times do I speak fear instead of faith? How many times do I show those around me that my belief in You is shallow simply because I give voice to my anxieties? Teach me to bridle my tongue and speak only confidence in Your love so I can help those who are hurting. I trust You completely, Father. Let my words and actions reflect that.

Pray First

*Is anyone among you suffering? Let him pray.
Is anyone cheerful? Let him sing praise. Is anyone
among you sick? Let him call for the elders of the
church, and let them pray over him, anointing him with
oil in the name of the Lord. And the prayer of faith will
save the one who is sick, and the Lord will raise him
up. And if he has committed sins, he will be forgiven.
Therefore, confess your sins to one another and pray
for one another, that you may be healed. The prayer
of a righteous person has great power as it is working.*
JAMES 5:13–16 ESV

Dear Father, I'm ashamed of how often I forget to pray. When someone I love faces hardship, I worry. When someone is sick, I fret, hoping things will get better. In the face of financial hardship or relationship troubles or so many other trials, I worry first. Teach me to pray first. I know prayer is the most powerful response to any situation.

Pray!

But even if you should suffer for righteousness' sake, you will be blessed. Have no fear of them, nor be troubled, but in your hearts honor Christ the Lord as holy, always being prepared to make a defense to anyone who asks you for a reason for the hope that is in you; yet do it with gentleness and respect, having a good conscience, so that, when you are slandered, those who revile your good behavior in Christ may be put to shame. For it is better to suffer for doing good, if that should be God's will, than for doing evil.
1 Peter 3:14–17 esv

Dear Father, worry changes nothing. Prayer changes everything. How often have I faced an impossible situation and, after declaring defeat, decided to pray? When will I learn? Prayer is never the *least* I can do. It's always the *most* I can do. It should be my first response, not my last resort. Forgive me for being such a slow learner. In all things, remind me to pray.

111

Claiming My Inheritance

His divine power has granted to us all things that pertain to life and godliness, through the knowledge of him who called us to his own glory and excellence, by which he has granted to us his precious and very great promises, so that through them you may become partakers of the divine nature, having escaped from the corruption that is in the world because of sinful desire.
2 Peter 1:3–4 esv

Dear Father, You've already given me everything I need to live a full, successful life by Your standards. But the way I claim this inheritance is through knowledge of Your Word. I can't claim Your promises unless I know what they are. Why do I worry about things when the answer to every question, the solution to every problem, is in Your Word? Teach me Your promises, Lord. Give me discipline to read Your Word so I can fully participate in the abundant life You have for me.

Have Patience

Do not overlook this one fact, beloved, that with the Lord one day is as a thousand years, and a thousand years as one day. The Lord is not slow to fulfill his promise as some count slowness, but is patient toward you, not wishing that any should perish, but that all should reach repentance.

2 PETER 3:8–9 ESV

Dear Father, sometimes my worry might actually be impatience. It's not that I don't believe You'll take care of things. It's that I think You're not acting according to my timeline. I want what I want, and I want it right now. I want You to hurry up. I'm a product of a fast-food, drive-through society, and my patience is limited. When I'm tempted to wring my hands, worry, and stress over things I can't control, remind me that You're already acting. Calm my spirit, and give me patience as I wait for Your best in all things.

Into the Light

This is the message we have heard from him and proclaim to you, that God is light, and in him is no darkness at all. If we say we have fellowship with him while we walk in darkness, we lie and do not practice the truth. But if we walk in the light, as he is in the light, we have fellowship with one another, and the blood of Jesus his Son cleanses us from all sin.

1 John 1:5–7 esv

Dear Father, Satan is called the Prince of Darkness. He is the embodiment of evil. When I listen to him, when I let worry and fear rule my thoughts, I'm inviting him into my inner circle. I'm pulling up a chair and asking him to make himself comfortable. I don't want Satan to be my buddy, Lord. Help me recognize fear as coming from him. Focus my thoughts on Your love, Your goodness, and Your hope. When I wander into darkness, pull me back into Your light. I trust You completely.

I Want to Know You More

By this we know that we have come to know him, if we keep his commandments. Whoever says "I know him" but does not keep his commandments is a liar, and the truth is not in him, but whoever keeps his word, in him truly the love of God is perfected. By this we may know that we are in him: whoever says he abides in him ought to walk in the same way in which he walked.

1 JOHN 2:3–6 ESV

. . . .

Dear Father, the way to grow a relationship is to spend time together. The only way I can really know You is to read Your Word and pray. When I worry, I choose to leave You out of my thoughts. Worry is actually a rejection of Your presence. The more I get to know Your promises and Your character, the more I realize that with You I have nothing to fear. Pull me into Your presence, Lord. I want to know You more.

The Birthright

*For everyone who has been born of God
overcomes the world. And this is the victory
that has overcome the world—our faith.*

1 John 5:4 esv

Dear Father, You created me to be a victor. I am designed to be an overcomer. It's my birthright as Your child. And the key to this birthright is my faith. Worry is a faith shrinker. It makes me into the victim instead of the victor. This life is like a race, and You want me to be a participant, not a spectator. You want me to dive right in, knowing the results are already recorded. I win! When I face life with faith instead of fear, I can't lose. When I was born into Your family, I was born a winner. Give me the faith and confidence fitting a child of the King, and teach me to act according to my birthright.

First Love

*"I know you are enduring patiently and bearing
up for my name's sake, and you have not grown
weary. But I have this against you, that you
have abandoned the love you had at first."*
REVELATION 2:3–4 ESV

Dear Father, when John addressed the church at Ephesus, he used some pretty stern words. He shared his observation that they had abandoned their first love. They had abandoned You! This breaks my heart, more for myself than for them. I know when I let worry control my thoughts, I'm doing the same thing the Ephesians did. I'm leaving my first love—You—for my fears.

There's one thing I've learned about You: You will only reside in first place. You are either Lord of all or You're not Lord at all. I want You to be Lord of my life, Father. Forgive me for pushing You aside in favor of my anxious thoughts. I love You more than anything. You are my first love, and I trust You completely.

Influencers

Blessed is the man who walks not in the counsel of the wicked, nor stands in the way of sinners, nor sits in the seat of scoffers; but his delight is in the law of the LORD, and on his law he meditates day and night.

PSALM 1:1–2 ESV

Dear Father, who influences my life? I know that the people I spend time with and the people I listen to will guide my thoughts. When I devote chunks of time to people who worry, I start to think like them. When I listen to negativity on TV or social media, my mind follows along. You've called me to a different way of life. You've called me to walk, talk, and think differently than the world. Fear is the world's way. Faith is Your way. When I'm overcome by fear, remind me that I'm not part of that crowd. Pull me into Your promises, and surround me with godly, faith-strong people. I want to be influenced by You alone.

Royal

*You, O Lord, are a shield about me, my glory,
and the lifter of my head. I cried aloud to the
Lord, and he answered me from his holy hill.*

PSALM 3:3–4 ESV

Dear Father, You lift my head. I don't need to walk in fear, shame, or anxiety. I am a child of the King! When I call, You always hear me, and You always answer. Whatever circumstance I face, I can leave it with You. You are always for me, never against me, and You will always act on my behalf. When worry tries to steal my sleep, remind me to call to You. When fear floods in, remind me that You are a shield around me, protecting me. When shame makes me doubt myself, my abilities, or my future, remind me that I'm Your child. Lift my head. Push my shoulders back. And teach me to walk like a member of Your royal family.

God's Child

But know that the LORD has set apart the godly
for himself; the LORD hears when I call to him.
PSALM 4:3 ESV

. . . .

Dear Father, when my son or daughter calls, I always answer the phone. When they want to talk, I listen with interest. Though I'm not a perfect parent, my love for them runs deep. How much greater is Your love for Your children? I can approach Your throne with confidence. I know You love me and will listen to every word I say with great interest. Worry no longer needs to be in my vocabulary. I can share any fear with You, and You will treat each concern with respect. You will take care of each need. You will comfort me through every storm. I'm so glad You chose me to be in Your family. Thank You for the peace that comes from being Your child.

Peaceful Sleep

*In peace I will both lie down and sleep; for you
alone, O LORD, make me dwell in safety.*
PSALM 4:8 ESV

. . . .

Dear Father, I've lost so many nights of sleep to worry. During the day, I'm pretty good at staying busy and distracting myself from my fears. But when I lie down, my brain wakes up. As soon as I try to sleep, worry has a party. Every negative thought tap-dances through my mind, and anxiety is the star of the show. I know that the best strategy to remove anxiety is prayer. Stay with me as I dissect those fears one by one and give them to You. Teach me to take every thought captive and lay it at Your feet, Lord. Give me Your peace. Give me rest. Remind me that You're strong and I'm safe. I trust You completely, and I know You'll take care of me.

Exchange Worry for Peace

*I am weary with my moaning; every night I
flood my bed with tears; I drench my couch with
my weeping. My eye wastes away because of
grief; it grows weak because of all my foes.*

PSALM 6:6–7 ESV

Dear Father, it's hard to believe King David wrote this. It could have come from my own pen. I know You've seen me cry myself to sleep. You've watched me turn my pillow to the dry side. You've witnessed me try, in vain, to cover my puffy eyes with makeup the next morning. I find comfort in knowing You see, You know, and You care. You've seen my tears for broken relationships. You've felt my heartache for those I love who are making poor choices. You've witnessed my fear over finances, my anxiety over health issues. Yet I know, just as David knew, that You are Lord of all. Take my worries, Lord, and exchange them for Your peace. I give it all to You.

Where Are You, Lord?

Why, O LORD, do you stand far away? Why do you hide yourself in times of trouble?
PSALM 10:1 ESV

· ·

Dear Father, I'm so glad David questioned You. You called him a man after Your own heart, and yet he made some pretty big mistakes in his life. Your hand was on him, but that didn't keep him from going through some wretched times. Here, he questioned You. He wanted to know where You were. I feel that way sometimes, Lord. I wonder why You're playing a game of hide-and-seek with me. I call out to You, but it feels like my prayers don't pass through the ceiling. Still, I know You're there, even when I don't feel You. I know You're working, even when I don't see anything happening. I need You, Abba Father. Show Yourself to me. Let me feel Your presence and Your peace.

Back to Praise

How long must I take counsel in my soul and have sorrow in my heart all the day? How long shall my enemy be exalted over me? . . . But I have trusted in your steadfast love; my heart shall rejoice in your salvation. I will sing to the LORD, because he has dealt bountifully with me.
PSALM 13:2, 5–6 ESV

Dear Father, David struggled with depression. He faced a lot of hardships in his life, and he walked through many days with fear and anxiety. But he always came back around to praising You. Conversation with You does that, doesn't it? When I praise You, when I lift You up, I get lifted up as well. You are bigger than my greatest fear. You are more powerful than my worst nightmare. Like David, I trust in Your steadfast love and rejoice in Your salvation. I will sing to You because You have been so, so good to me.

Your Goodness

You make known to me the path of life;
you will fill me with joy in your presence,
with eternal pleasures at your right hand.

PSALM 16:11 NIV

. . . .

Dear Father, You are so good to me. I look back on my life, and I see clearly that Your love has stayed with me. Your presence has been a constant from my earliest memories. Even when I didn't feel You there in the moment, I can see now that You were never far away. You were right there beside me, protecting me, comforting me, and guiding me. You've never given me any reason to worry about my future. I don't know why my thoughts automatically home in on the worst outcomes, when Your kindness has always gone before me and behind me. Thank You for Your goodness, Your love, and Your peace. I trust You completely in every detail of my life.

125

Inhale and Exhale

You have delivered me from the attacks of the people; you have made me the head of nations. People I did not know now serve me.

PSALM 18:43 NIV

. . . .

Dear Father, You know how I worry about the future. I want to know with certainty what will happen, and I get scared when things don't play out the way I want them to. If anyone had a reason to worry, it was David. He went through difficult situations, but You delivered him every time. You lifted him up and set him in a place of honor. You tend to do that with Your children who love You. Father, I know You've never promised smooth seas. Right now I'm in a storm, but I will exhale my fears and inhale Your peace, knowing You will deliver me. I have confidence that in the end You will set me in a place of honor.

126

Meditations

May these words of my mouth and this meditation of my heart be pleasing in your sight, LORD, my Rock and my Redeemer.
PSALM 19:14 NIV

. . . .

Dear Father, I want my thoughts and my words to please You. Yet I can be double-minded. I tend to focus on the negative instead of on You. I can't control the thoughts that go through my mind, but I can control which ones I meditate on. I can control which ones I talk about. When worrisome thoughts try to roost in my brain, help me shoo them away. Pull my thoughts to Your goodness, Your kindness, and Your love. Fill my spirit with Your presence, and hold an ongoing conversation with me. When I speak, let those words glorify You and bless those around me. You truly are my Rock and my Redeemer, and I want to praise You all day, every day of my life.

Where Is My Trust?

Some trust in chariots and some in horses,
but we trust in the name of the LORD our God.
They are brought to their knees and fall,
but we rise up and stand firm.
PSALM 20:7–8 NIV

Dear Father, in Bible times, people trusted in mighty armies to protect them. If their horses got sick or their chariots caught on fire, they were terrified. The source of their confidence could be wiped out in an instant. Today, this verse might read "Some trust in money, success, or fame; some trust in health or relationships. . ." The truth about this kind of confidence still stands. Money, job stability, success—it can be taken away in an instant. As long as my trust is in fallible, worldly people or things, I'm in danger. But when I place full confidence in You, that trust will never fail me. Father, all my trust is in You. I know that as long as my confidence is in You, in the end I will stand.

Justice for All, Every Time

*Your hand will lay hold on all your enemies;
your right hand will seize your foes. When you
appear for battle, you will burn them up as in a
blazing furnace. The LORD will swallow them up
in his wrath, and his fire will consume them.*

PSALM 21:8–9 NIV

Dear Father, contrary to common belief, You don't have any political affiliation. You have no country. You will bless the righteous and curse the wicked—period. People who seek Your wisdom and live by Your righteousness will be blessed. People who skulk about and try to manipulate or who lie and cheat for personal gain ultimately will be found out and punished. You see all. You know all. And You have everything handled. Forgive me for worrying that things won't work out the way they're supposed to. I trust You to see justice done in every situation. Thank You for the peace that comes from knowing You're in control.

God's Address

*Oh my God, I cry by day, but you do not answer,
and by night, but I find no rest. Yet you are
holy, enthroned on the praises of Israel.*

PSALM 22:2–3 ESV

Dear Father, once again, David has accurately captured my own thoughts and emotions. Where are You? Why aren't You listening? My soul cries out to You, but it doesn't feel like You hear me at all. I have so many worries, so many concerns that weigh me down. Why aren't You answering me? Yet, I know the truth. I know where You live. You gave me Your address right here in this verse. You are enthroned on the praises of Your people. When I praise You, I'm there. When I lift You up, I'm immediately in Your presence. Thank You for this reminder that when I feel far from You, all I need to do is praise You. You will be right there.

Refreshed

He refreshes my soul. He guides me along the right paths for his name's sake. . . . Surely your goodness and love will follow me all the days of my life, and I will dwell in the house of the LORD forever.

PSALM 23:3, 6 NIV

Dear Father, You refresh my soul. This passage indicates that I'll need to be refreshed. Life will wear me down and deplete my strength. Another translation (ESV) says that You restore my soul. Regardless of the circumstances, regardless of what's in my past, You will restore. You will refresh. You will make me new again. David said, "Surely your goodness and love will follow me all the days of my life." It's true. Your goodness chases me. You pursue me so You can pour out love, kindness, peace, and joy on my life. I can't fathom that kind of love, but I'm so grateful for it, Father. I want to dwell in Your presence every day of my life.

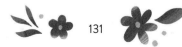

Hope in You

No one who hopes in you will ever be put to shame, but shame will come on those who are treacherous without cause.

PSALM 25:3 NIV

. . . .

Dear Father, the word *hope* means to wait in expectation of something good. When we're patient and wait on Your timing, it always pays off. But I'm not great at the waiting part, Lord. Like a little child, I want what I want, and I want it now. I get anxious and worried when You don't deliver the goods right away. Help me calm down and wait on You. Forgive me for trying to control the situation and force things to happen on my timeline. I know Your plan is so much better than anything I can bring about on my own. I will wait for You, Father, with confidence that You have something wonderful in store. You've never failed me, and You never will.

Friendship with God

The friendship of the LORD is for those who
fear him, and he makes known to them his
covenant. My eyes are ever toward the LORD,
for he will pluck my feet out of the net.
PSALM 25:14–15 ESV

Dear Father, I want to be Your friend! I want You to confide in me. I want us to spend time together, laughing and talking, singing and playing. I know this kind of close relationship comes through my reverence for You. It comes through my faith that You will keep Your promises. Be my Friend, Father. Hold my hand. Calm my fears. Share Your presence with me. I want to feel Your joy and experience Your peace. I want the confidence of knowing that no matter what I may walk into, You are right there with me, holding my hand, supporting me with Your strength. I have never had a friend like You, Father, and I'm so grateful that You want to be close to me. Thank You for being my Friend.

Rescue Me

*Guard my life and rescue me; do not let
me be put to shame, for I take refuge in
you. May integrity and uprightness protect
me, because my hope, Lord, is in you.*
PSALM 25:20–21 NIV

. . . .

Dear Father, You don't need me to lay all my concerns before You. You already know every thought, every fear. But here I am, anyway. I need this conversation, this connection with You. I need You to rescue me, Father. I need You to rescue those I love. Like a child afraid of the storm, I need You to be my refuge. I want to crawl up in Your lap, feel Your strong arms around me, and place my face in Your neck. Father, You know my heart. You know I long to please You. Because of that, I beg You, Lord. Be my Protector. You are my only hope, and I know it's not a misplaced hope. I know You will deliver me out of this storm to a good and peaceful place.

Confident

I remain confident of this: I will see the goodness of the LORD in the land of the living. Wait for the LORD; be strong and take heart and wait for the LORD.
PSALM 27:13–14 NIV

. . . .

Dear Father, I love this passage. I love David's confidence in You. He knew he would see good things while he was still alive. His wasn't just a distant hope of a distant place called heaven, though that hope is just as real and exciting as anything I can imagine. Your goodness is for this life. It's for right here, right now. But there's that hard word again. . .*wait*. Like a child waiting for Christmas, I'm impatient. I don't want to have to wait. Patience isn't one of my strengths, Lord. Yet, like David, I have confidence in Your goodness. I will be strong. I will take heart. I know that one day You will pour out Your goodness on me and on those I love, and I will be overwhelmed. I can't wait.

Praise the Lord!

Praise be to the LORD, for he has heard my cry for mercy. The LORD is my strength and my shield; my heart trusts in him, and he helps me. My heart leaps for joy, and with my song I praise him.

PSALM 28:6–7 NIV

Dear Father, worry wears me down. It steals my joy. But worry and fear over the future do not control me. Instead of worry, I choose to praise You! Instead of fear, I choose to relax into Your presence. I will fall into Your love, knowing Your strength will support me. You are my protection, my refuge, my safe place. I trust You completely, Father. It's amazing. A minute ago I was worried and defeated. But now, Your joy has filled me up! I will praise You and praise You and praise You, Father. I know You are good and You will take care of me.

In the Flood

The Lord sits enthroned over the flood; the Lord is enthroned as King forever. The Lord gives strength to his people; the Lord blesses his people with peace.
PSALM 29:10–11 NIV

. . . .

Dear Father, rain is a good thing. It brings nourishment to the soil and makes the crops plentiful. Rain is a blessing, but a flood is never a good thing. A flood brings destruction. Right now, I feel like I'm drowning, and I need You to rescue me. I feel weak and defeated, and I'm not sure if I can make it through. I reach up to You, knowing You are enthroned over this flood. You are all-powerful and almighty, and I trust You to lift me out of this mess. I feel Your strength infusing my spirit right now, Father. I feel Your peace covering me. Thank You for being God in times of blessing and during the flood.

Joy in the Morning

Sing the praises of the LORD, you his faithful people;
praise his holy name. For his anger lasts only a
moment, but his favor lasts a lifetime; weeping may
stay for the night, but rejoicing comes in the morning.
PSALM 30:4–5 NIV

Dear Father, I know I bring about some of my own bad circumstances. I make poor choices, and those decisions come with consequences. But I also know You love me. Right now, I'm in a dark place. I feel like I've cried all my tears, but they just keep coming. Still, I will praise You. Even if it feels like there's nothing else good in my life, *You* are good. I know You will never leave me or forsake me. I need Your touch, Father. I need to feel Your presence, Your kindness, Your love. Give me Your peace, and let me experience Your joy. My hope is in You, Father. In the midst of this storm, I praise You. I know You have good things in store.

Mourning to Dancing

You turned my wailing into dancing; you removed
my sackcloth and clothed me with joy, that my
heart may sing your praises and not be silent.
Lord my God, I will praise you forever.
Psalm 30:11–12 niv

Dear Father, I know You feel every tear I shed. You are compassionate, which means You experience my pain, my worries, and my fears right along with me. You know I'm mourning the loss of things that are important to me. You know how my heart breaks over my relationships, over job loss, over financial strain. You feel every bit of my pain. But that's where the story takes a turn, isn't it? You don't just feel my heartbreak. . .You take it from me. You turn my mourning into dancing. You take away my desperation and fill me with Your joy. Father, I will praise You until I feel those beautiful traits bubbling out of me. And then, I'll praise You some more. I will praise You forever.

When Relationships Are Hard

*Oh, how abundant is your goodness, which
you have stored up for those who fear you and
worked for those who take refuge in you, in the sight
of the children of mankind! In the cover of your
presence you hide them from the plots of men; you
store them in your shelter from the strife of tongues.*
PSALM 31:19–20 ESV

. . . .

Dear Father, relationships are hard. I know You intended them to be a blessing, but they can be the source of such deep pain. Help me to never be a source of sorrow for others. Let my words be kind and positive and encouraging. Let my actions be a blessing instead of a curse. When others speak against me, shield me. Protect me from the pain of their words. Guard me from their deceit, their schemes, and their plots. Be my refuge. Protect my emotions, and fill me with Your peace.

To the Brink

Praise be to the LORD, for he showed me the wonders of his love when I was in a city under siege. In my alarm I said, "I am cut off from your sight!" Yet you heard my cry for mercy when I called to you for help.
PSALM 31:21–22 NIV

Dear Father, I'm so glad David wrote down his experiences so the rest of us can benefit. In those moments when he knew he'd be overtaken, You rescued him. You really do enjoy those grand gestures, don't You, Father? At times, You allow us to be taken to the brink to test our faith and to set up a great victory. But no matter what happens, no matter how bad things get, I know You are faithful. I know You won't let me down. I trust You, and I can't wait to see how You pull me out of this. I am confident You will deliver me and this ending will be good.

Take Heart

*Love the LORD, all his faithful people! The LORD
preserves those who are true to him, but the
proud he pays back in full. Be strong and
take heart, all you who hope in the LORD.*
PSALM 31:23–24 NIV

Dear Father, You love that word *hope*, don't You? You tell those who hope in You—those who believe that You have good things in store for their lives—to be strong. To take heart. To hang in there because the blessings are on the way. Forgive me for doubting You, Father. Forgive me for worrying, for believing my worst fears will destroy me. Give me faith. Give me confidence in Your love. I know You see everything I'm going through right now. You haven't missed a thing. You already know my fears, but I give them to You. I trust You completely. You are my hope, and I know You won't fail.

Wait in Hope

We wait in hope for the LORD; he is our help and our shield. In him our hearts rejoice, for we trust in his holy name.

PSALM 33:20–21 NIV

Dear Father, so many times in scripture You encourage me to wait. Too often, I try to move ahead of You. I talk to You about my needs and desires, and I might wait a hot minute . . .but if You don't answer my question or solve my problem right away, I take it all back. I begin to manipulate and scheme instead of just resting in You. Forgive me for my impatience, Lord. Teach me to wait. Distract me with Your goodness, and help me distract myself with praise, with love for others, and with acts of service. I've poured out my heart to You, Father. Now I'll wait, I'll trust You, and I'll rejoice in expectation of Your goodness.

Ruled by Hope

May your unfailing love be with us, LORD,
even as we put our hope in you.
PSALM 33:22 NIV

Dear Father, that word *hope* is a constant reminder to me of the way I should live my life. Hope is the belief that good things are coming. Do I live in hope? Too often, I'm ruled by fear. I think of the worst possible scenario, and my thoughts just sit there. I'm learning that fear is a choice. Why do I let it control me? I don't have to pay any more attention to a worrisome thought than to a buzzing mosquito. I can slap it away, and *splat!* It's gone. When I choose to focus on worry instead of on Your love for me, I waste so many breaths. Forgive me for succumbing to fear. Shower me with Your love, Lord. My hope is in You.

Seek Peace

Come, my children, listen to me; I will teach you
the fear of the LORD. Whoever of you loves life and
desires to see many good days, keep your tongue
from evil and your lips from telling lies. Turn from
evil and do good; seek peace and pursue it.

PSALM 34:11–14 NIV

. . . .

Dear Father, Your Word is so clear. You tell me exactly what I need to do to have an abundant, peaceful life. I need to keep my tongue from evil and my lips from speaking lies. I need to turn from evil and do good, to seek peace and pursue it. When I give voice to my worries, I'm really speaking lies. Satan wants to form my circumstances into fear, and he is the father of lies. You, on the other hand, promise only hope. Help me turn from the evil of Satan's deceptive, worrisome thoughts. Help me distract myself by chasing after goodness, by seeking Your peace. I know I'll find exactly what I'm looking for.

Just Enough

Better the little that the righteous have
than the wealth of many wicked.

PSALM 37:16 NIV

. . . .

Dear Father, when I look at celebrities on social media, I often think about how nice it would be to have that kind of money. But when I take a closer look at their lives, I realize a wealthy lifestyle can be stressful. Those people don't always know who their friends are because some people use them for their money. They often get caught up in having more: more money, bigger houses, more expensive boats and cars. But those things don't bring joy or peace. Those things can't love you back. Help me see the blessing and peace that come from having just enough. Remind me to focus on people, not things. Remind me to notice the quiet extravagances, like a gorgeous sunset or a wildflower in bloom. Thank You for Your generosity, and thank You for Your peace.

Stronghold

*The salvation of the righteous comes from
the LORD; he is their stronghold in time of
trouble. The LORD helps them and delivers them;
he delivers them from the wicked and saves
them, because they take refuge in him.*
PSALM 37:39–40 NIV

. . . .

Dear Father, a stronghold is a place that has been fortified
to protect it against attack—like a castle with stone walls
and moats built around it to protect whatever's inside the
walls. I can't think of a better, more powerful stronghold
than You, Lord. I belong to You, and You've set Yourself
around me as my protection. With You on my side, nothing
can overcome me! I may get scratched now and then, but
that's expected in battle. I can confidently face anything
life throws at me. I know You will protect me, and I'll come
through it stronger than ever.

A Wisp

"Show me, LORD, my life's end and the number of my days; let me know how fleeting my life is. You have made my days a mere handbreadth; the span of my years is as nothing before you. Everyone is but a breath, even those who seem secure. Surely everyone goes around like a mere phantom; in vain they rush about, heaping up wealth without knowing whose it will finally be."

PSALM 39:4–6 NIV

Dear Father, why do I worry about wealth, success, or status? Those things are temporary. What does it matter, anyway? My life is nothing more than a wisp. Why do I waste even a moment trying to acquire things that won't last? Father, may my wisp of time please You. May my short vapor of a life bring delight to Your heart. That is all I exist for, Lord. I love You.

Self-Talk

*Why, my soul, are you downcast? Why so
disturbed within me? Put your hope in God,
for I will yet praise him, my Savior and my God.
My soul is downcast within me; therefore I will
remember you from the land of the Jordan,
the heights of Hermon—from Mount Mizar.*

PSALM 42:5–6 NIV

Dear Father, I love that the author of this psalm talked to himself. I do that all the time. But too often, my self-talk is negative. Instead of having a pep talk, I discourage myself. I feed my fears and nurture my anxieties. But this writer knew the importance of positive self-talk. Help me follow his example as I ask myself, *What are you so upset about? Why are you worried? God is your hope. He has it all under control.* When the negative voices in my head shout, draw me to Your whisper. Remind me of Your goodness, mercy, and love. My hope is in You.

149

God Is within Me

God is within her, she will not fall;
God will help her at break of day.
PSALM 46:5 NIV

. . . .

Dear Father, I know this verse isn't talking about a woman. It refers to Your holy city and how You'll protect Your people. Still, when I read this, I like to think of myself. After all, You live inside me. You give me strength. Since my power and courage come from You, I'm just as strong and steadfast as You are. I don't need to worry. I don't need to be anxious. I have nothing to fear. You are right here, living and breathing within me. Thank You for handling every problem that comes my way. I trust You completely. When I feel overwhelmed and afraid, bring Your words to mind, personalized just for me. *God is within me, I will not fall; God will help me at break of day.*

Be Still and Know

*He says, "Be still, and know that I am
God; I will be exalted among the nations,
I will be exalted in the earth."*
PSALM 46:10 NIV

Dear Father, why is it so hard for me to be still? When life comes at me full force and worries push in, I want to feel like I'm in control. I panic, thinking I need to do something—anything—to change the trajectory of my circumstance. But like a parent calming a frantic child, You shush me. Deep in my spirit I hear You whisper, "Be still." I feel Your heartbeat pulse in time with my own, reassuring me that You are still on Your throne, still in control. Help me quiet my thoughts and focus on You alone. I know You love me, You are kind, and You will work everything out for good.

The Mighty One

The Mighty One, God the L<small>ORD</small>, speaks and summons the earth from the rising of the sun to its setting.

P<small>SALM</small> 50:1 ESV

. . . .

Dear Father, Your power and resources are limitless. I don't know why I worry about anything, because I'm Your daughter and an heir with Christ. It's not logical for me to try to work things out on my own, because without You, my resources are limited. Thank You for this reminder of Your power, Your might, and the scope of Your control. Just as You speak and control the sun, the moon, and the earth, I know You control my circumstances. Even when I don't understand the course of events, I know I can trust Your goodness and Your love for me. Speak now, Father. Command the events that steal my sleep. And as I wait for You to work things out, I will praise You.

Thank You

"The one who offers thanksgiving as his sacrifice glorifies me; to one who orders his way rightly I will show the salvation of God!"
PSALM 50:23 ESV

. . . .

Dear Father, I know I'm supposed to thank You in all circumstances. Truly, You've given me so many things to be thankful for. But when the hard things in life crowd in, I forget. Remind me, Lord, that when times get tough, I need to thank You. I need to praise You. I need to list all the countless things You've done for me, all the beautiful gifts You send me each day. My thoughts need to live in that place. Thank You for Your love. Thank You for Your Son. Thank You for my family and for friends who feel like family. Thank You for food to eat, clothes to wear, and shelter. Thank You for the beautiful sunrise and sunset each day. Thank You for inhabiting the air I breathe and for wrapping me in Your presence. Thank You, Father, for Your kindness to me.

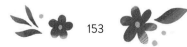

You've Never Failed

For he has delivered me from every trouble, and
my eye has looked in triumph on my enemies.
PSALM 54:7 ESV

. . . .

Dear Father, this verse brings to mind that old saying "Hindsight is twenty-twenty." As I look back on my life, I can see clearly that You've never let me down. You've brought me through every trial and stood with me through storms and fires. When people have been cruel, You've sheltered me, comforted me, and brought me to a good place despite their intentions. Even in the worst of times, You've showered me with love and kindness. Why is Your love so clear in hindsight, but foresight seems so blurry? When I face the future, I worry. I feel afraid. Instead of letting me listen to my fears, let me draw faith from my experience with You. You've never once failed me. And I know You never will.

 154

Not Afraid

*Be gracious to me, O God, for man tramples
on me; all day long an attacker oppresses me;
my enemies trample on me all day long, for many
attack me proudly. When I am afraid, I put my trust
in you. In God, whose word I praise, in God I trust;
I shall not be afraid. What can flesh do to me?*
PSALM 56:1–4 ESV

Dear Father, right now, I feel that life is trampling me. Like David, I feel pursued. It's hard not to panic in those situations. But like David, I will trust You. Let me feel Your presence now, Father. Calm me, and help me breathe. Bring songs of praise and thanksgiving to mind. I know praise escorts me into Your throne room, and that's where I need to be right now. I feel safe in Your presence, so that's where I'll stay. I trust You. I will not be afraid.

I Cry Out

I cry out to God Most High, to God who fulfills his purpose for me. He will send from heaven and save me; he will put to shame him who tramples on me. God will send out his steadfast love and his faithfulness!
PSALM 57:2–3 ESV

Dear Father, I know You don't cause the bad things in my life. But sometimes I wonder if You allow them because You miss me and You want me to run into Your arms. Right now, I cry out to You. You know my circumstances. You're aware of every hurt, every need, every longing of my heart. Even as I pray, I feel my heartbeat slowing, and I feel a calm and a peace I didn't feel before. I know You're on Your way! I know You will rescue me, Father. I have confidence in Your love for me. Thank You for Your faithfulness.

Sing!

But I will sing of your strength; I will sing aloud of your steadfast love in the morning. For you have been to me a fortress and a refuge in the day of my distress. O my Strength, I will sing praises to you, for you, O God, are my fortress, the God who shows me steadfast love.
PSALM 59:16–17 ESV

· ·

Dear Father, when I feel overwhelmed, I freeze. I don't know what to do other than wring my hands and worry. But worry doesn't have any power to make things better. It only makes things worse. When I'm about to get bogged down in my fear and anxiety, remind me to sing! I will sing Your praises, for praise ushers me into Your presence. I will sing out loud, for music has a way of calming my spirit. And when I can't sing aloud, I'll sing in my heart, in my spirit. I'll hum. With each breath, with each stanza, I'll remember who You are. And I'll remember that I belong to You.

With You

*Oh, grant us help against the foe, for vain is
the salvation of man! With God we shall do
valiantly; it is he who will tread down our foes.*
Psalm 60:11–12 esv

Dear Father, I am nothing without You. Without You, I will undoubtedly fail. But with You, I am a victor! With You, I'm a mighty warrior. I am brave and strong and powerful. I can do all things through You for You are my strength. With You by my side, I cannot fail. Sometimes I look at my problems and realize there's no way I can overcome them. I feel doomed. But then I remember I'm not alone. I have You right beside me, fighting from within me. With You, I can move mountains. I can conquer armies. With You, I will overcome. Thank You for the confidence, joy, and peace that come from knowing You.

Not Greatly Shaken

*For God alone my soul waits in silence; from him
comes my salvation. He alone is my rock and my
salvation, my fortress; I shall not be greatly shaken.*
PSALM 62:1–2 ESV

Dear Father, there's that word again: *wait*. David wrote that his soul waits in silence. This gives me the idea that he was calm. He wasn't frantic or panicked or worried. Teach me to wait in calm, in silence, Lord. He also said that he will not be greatly shaken. He didn't say he wouldn't be shaken. Life shakes us sometimes. It tosses us about, and sometimes we lose our balance. But with You, I won't be *greatly* shaken. In other words, I'll be fine. I'll come through this circumstance with only a few scratches and a great story to tell. You are my rock, Father. You are my fortress. Thank You for protecting me even in the earthquakes.

Pray, Don't Panic

Trust in him at all times, O people; pour out your heart before him; God is a refuge for us.

PSALM 62:8 ESV

Dear Father, I don't know why my go-to response is panic. Even when nothing has gone wrong, my mind floats to everything that *could* go wrong, and I sit there. Yet I have no reason to worry. You've never let me down. You've always taken care of me. You've given me everything I need, plus many things I don't really need but I want. You're generous and kind. When my mind sinks into worry, when my spirit goes into panic mode, remind me of Your love. Invite me into the refuge of Your presence, and remind me that, unlike panic, prayer really does change things. Like David in this psalm, I will pour out my heart to You. And I will trust Your goodness.

Satisfied

*My soul will be satisfied as with fat and rich food,
and my mouth will praise you with joyful lips, when I
remember you upon my bed, and meditate on you in
the watches of the night; for you have been my help,
and in the shadow of your wings I will sing for joy.
My soul clings to you; your right hand upholds me.*
PSALM 63:5–8 ESV

. . . .

Dear Father, it's all about focus, isn't it? I can set my mind on worry, or I can set my mind on praise. I've noticed that when I praise You, my fears dissipate. When I praise You, joy seeps in and fills up every crack, every crevice, of my spirit. Despite the hard things I've faced, You have been so, so good to me. Like David, I am so satisfied, so *stuffed* with Your goodness. Like an infant clinging to her parent for safety and protection, I will cling to You, Father. And I will rejoice in Your amazing, overwhelming love for me.

Don't Worry; Be Happy!

*Let the righteous one rejoice in the LORD and take
refuge in him! Let all the upright in heart exult!*

PSALM 64:10 ESV

. . . .

Dear Father, as I read this verse, for some reason I hear
that old song "Don't Worry; Be Happy!" in my head. You
don't want Your children to worry about anything, do You?
You want us to be happy. You want us to rejoice in You.
When I'm afraid, I can always run to You, for in Your presence I'll find safety and joy and peace. No matter what I
face, I can be confident that You have my back. You have
my front and my sides too. You hem me in, providing a
shelter that Satan can't penetrate. Satan wants me to
worry. But today, I choose to be happy. I will rejoice in You
and in Your great love for me.

He Listens

*But truly God has listened; he has attended
to the voice of my prayer. Blessed be God,
because he has not rejected my prayer or
removed his steadfast love from me!*
PSALM 66:19–20 ESV

. . . .

Dear Father, I know I'm not supposed to worry. But I also know I can talk to You about my worries and You won't condemn me. Instead, You'll pull me onto Your lap, comfort me, and tell me I came to the right place. You'll assure me that You love me and that You'll take care of me. Thank You for listening, Father, even when I share the same fears I've shared a hundred times before. Build my faith and make me strong. Thank You for the peace that comes from knowing You're on my side. When I'm afraid, remind me to come to You, talk to You, and praise You for Your goodness.

Save Me!

Save me, O God! For the waters have come up to my neck. I sink in deep mire, where there is no foothold; I have come into deep waters, and the flood sweeps over me. I am weary with my crying out; my throat is parched. My eyes grow dim with waiting for my God.
PSALM 69:1–3 ESV

Dear Father, so many of David's prayers could have been written today. I can apply these words to our nation, our government, our world. I can apply them to my health and finances. They eloquently speak to my fears for my children and others I love. So much evil is present in this world, and it seems to be getting worse. Yet I know who will save me. I know whom to run to in these times. I will wait for You, knowing You will come to my rescue. I'll keep calling to You, for You are my only hope. And I will praise You because I know Your power and I know Your love.

Please Hurry!

O God, be not far from me;
O my God, make haste to help me!
PSALM 71:12 ESV

Dear Father, I know You're never far away, but sometimes it feels like You are. Sometimes it feels like I'm facing the giants alone. I know I'm supposed to wait for You, but God, please hurry! I desperately need You to act. Even in the waiting, Lord, I trust You. This life is full of troubles, but I know You love me and will see me through them all. Even in the worst storm, I am not without hope. With You, there is always the promise of a better tomorrow both in this life and in the one to come. Let me feel Your presence, Father. Remind me that You're here and that You're working on my behalf. I love You, I trust You, and I know You are good.

Focus Outward

Our king helps the poor who cry out to him—those in need who have no one to help them. He feels sorry for all who are weak and poor. He protects their lives. He saves them from the cruel people who try to hurt them. Their lives are important to him.

PSALM 72:12–14 ERV

Dear Father, I can apply this passage to my own life, knowing You will rescue me. But I can also use it as a call to action. Sometimes I worry because I have too much time on my hands. Give me Your eyes, Father. Show me the people around me who need help. Show me those who need Your love, and let me be the delivery girl for Your compassion and kindness. When I turn my focus outward, my faith grows. My fears are calmed. And my spirit is flooded with the joy and peace that come from living out Your purpose.

Near God

But for me it is good to be near God; I have made the Lord GOD my refuge, that I may tell of all your works.
PSALM 73:28 ESV

. . . .

Dear Father, You truly are my refuge. I love You so much. Recently, my life has been crazy and scary, and I find myself worrying a lot. But I know You are with me always, even in this difficult time. You have blessed me with so many things—yet it's easy to forget those kindnesses when I'm focused on my fears. You've given me family and friends. You've given me air to breathe, food to eat, and clothes to wear. You've provided shelter. I know that even when it seems like everything is going wrong, You are there, pouring out Your love on my life. More than anything, I want to stay close to You, Father, because that's where I'll find security, love, and peace.

Valley of Weeping

Blessed are those whose strength is in you, in whose heart are the highways to Zion. As they go through the Valley of Baca they make it a place of springs; the early rain also covers it with pools. They go from strength to strength; each one appears before God in Zion.

PSALM 84:5–7 ESV

Dear Father, I looked up "Valley of Baca." It means "Valley of Weeping." How appropriate. I'm there, Father. I'm at the end of myself, the end of my strength, the end of my ability to deal with my circumstances. But that's where the blessings are, right? When I'm empty, You fill me. When I'm hungry, You satisfy me. When I'm broken, You pick up the pieces and put them back together in a work of art that's more beautiful than anything I could have imagined. I don't like it here, in the Valley of Weeping. But I love knowing I'm not alone. I feel Your presence, and I know You're doing something good.

I'm Listening

Let me hear what God the LORD will speak, for he will speak peace to his people, to his saints; but let them not turn back to folly. Surely his salvation is near to those who fear him, that glory may dwell in our land.

PSALM 85:8–9 ESV

Dear Father, let me hear You! I need You to speak peace over my life. I know my worry is the folly the psalmist spoke of. Worry doesn't do any good, and it steals my joy and robs me of my sleep. Pull me away from those thoughts, Father, and turn my musings to Your goodness. Remind me that You are almighty and all-powerful. Remind me that You command every circumstance and that I have nothing to fear. Talk to me, Father. Whisper. Shout. Do whatever You need to do to get my attention. I want to hear what You have to say. I'm listening, and I'm Yours.

Triggers

I will sing of the steadfast love of the Lord,
forever; with my mouth I will make known
your faithfulness to all generations.
Psalm 89:1 esv

Dear Father, I have wasted so much of my life worrying about things that never happened. From now on, I want to be more productive with my time. I want to use worry as a trigger, a reminder to do something else. Today, when I worry about anything, I'll sing a praise song or hymn instead. (I might even take the opportunity to write my own song to You.) Today, when I'm tempted to worry, I'll tell someone how great You are. I'll talk about Your faithfulness in my life. Today, when fear pushes in, I'll find a way to serve You by serving other people. I'll show someone a kindness or speak an encouraging word. Thank You for these triggers, Father. Help me use them well.

Because She's Mine

"Because he holds fast to me in love, I will deliver him;
I will protect him, because he knows my name. When
he calls to me, I will answer him; I will be with him in
trouble; I will rescue him and honor him. With long
life I will satisfy him and show him my salvation."
PSALM 91:14–16 ESV

. . . .

Dear Father, I love this passage that's written from Your point of view. Your love doesn't have anything to do with my actions. I don't have to earn it, and I certainly don't deserve it. You pour Your love out on me simply because I belong to You. You look at me and say, "That one's Mine." You come to my rescue every time I call. I don't know why it's so hard for me to get it through my thick skull—I'm Your child. And because of that, You'll always take care of me.

Flourish

*The righteous flourish like the palm tree and grow
like a cedar in Lebanon. They are planted in the house
of the L*ord*; they flourish in the courts of our God.
They still bear fruit in old age; they are ever full of
sap and green, to declare that the L*ord *is upright; he
is my rock, and there is no unrighteousness in him.*

Psalm 92:12–15 esv

Dear Father, I'm not flourishing. It seems I'm passed over at every turn, like my value has diminished. Sometimes I feel like one of those gophers in the arcade game; I get bopped every time I stick my head up. Even so, I trust You. I know You are wise. You don't make mistakes. You are good and kind. When I don't understand what You're doing, I will trust in Your love for me. And I know one of these days I'll look around and realize You've watered my spirit all along. One day, I will flourish. I know I will because You promised it.

When I Can't Feel You

Hear my prayer, O LORD; let my cry come to you! Do not hide your face from me in the day of my distress! Incline your ear to me; answer me speedily in the day when I call!
PSALM 102:1–2 ESV

. . . .

Dear Father, You promised to never leave me. You promised You would never forsake me. But right now, I feel alone. I feel forsaken. Right now, I'm running on faith. I'm operating on Your promises because I don't feel Your presence. Please listen to me, Father! Hear me. Answer me. Do something to let me know You're still here. Yet even in my desperation, I know I can fall back on Your love for me. I don't know what You're doing, and I don't like it at all. But I will stay. I will keep looking for You. And I will trust in Your love.

Not an Orphan

*As a father shows compassion to his children, so the
Lord shows compassion to those who fear him.*
Psalm 103:13 esv

Dear Father, in my head, I know I belong to You. In my head, I know You are a good, good Father. But my actions often revert to orphan status. Despite having Your stamp and seal on my life, despite having Your Holy Spirit with me every day, despite all You've done for me. . .I operate out of fear. I act like I must do it all on my own, and that terrifies me. Don't give up on me, Lord. Remind me that I belong to You. Remind me that You are my loving, compassionate Father and that You will take care of me. Keep pulling me into Your presence, and show me Your kindness and grace. You are my Father and I am Your child, and I know that will never change.

Facing Illness

"If you will diligently listen to the voice of the LORD your God, and do that which is right in his eyes, and give ear to his commandments and keep all his statutes, I will put none of the diseases on you that I put on the Egyptians, for I am the LORD, your healer."

EXODUS 15:26 ESV

Dear Father, I know this verse isn't a promise that if I live perfectly in Your will, I'll never get sick. I live in a fallen, broken world, and unfortunately, disease is a part of that. Still, I know Your ways are always best. When I choose to listen to Your Word and follow Your precepts, there is a measure of protection. When I live a quiet, godly life, when I don't put harmful things in my body, when I exercise wisdom and discretion in my actions, I avoid many of life's pitfalls. But even when health problems find me, I will trust You, knowing You will work everything out for my good.

Provider

"The LORD will open to you his good treasury, the heavens, to give the rain to your land in its season and to bless all the work of your hands. And you shall lend to many nations, but you shall not borrow."

DEUTERONOMY 28:12 ESV

Dear Father, I know my bank account isn't tied to my salary or an earthly inheritance. Instead, it's connected to Your riches! I often worry about how I'll pay my bills, how I'll buy my groceries, and how I'll provide for my family. I know You expect me to be wise with the resources You've given me. Teach me moderation and self-control where it's needed. Beyond that, I won't worry about where the money will come from. I will trust You and wait with anticipation to see how You'll work. I know You will provide. You've never failed me, and I know You never will.

The Love of Money

He who loves money will not be satisfied
with money, nor he who loves wealth
with his income; this also is vanity.
ECCLESIASTES 5:10 ESV

Dear Father, I've often equated the love of money with big houses, fancy cars, and expensive clothes. But the thing I love most is the thing I spend the most time thinking about. I probably spend too much time thinking about money. I worry about retirement. I worry about how I'll pay for my children's education. I worry that there won't be enough for whatever may come. All that worry adds up to a lot of time thinking about money. Even when I have enough to meet one goal, there's always something else, always a need for more. Retrain my mind, Father. Teach me to trust You for today. Teach me to leave tomorrow's needs in Your hands. When money dominates my thoughts, draw my attention to You. I know You will supply all my needs according to Your riches.

Protection

*For wisdom is protection just as money is
protection, but the advantage of knowledge
is that wisdom keeps its possessors alive.*
ECCLESIASTES 7:12 NASB

Dear Father, I depend on money for security: security from health issues, security in old age, security for whatever may come. But money can't protect me from disease. Money can't extend my life. It can be taken away in an instant. The security I feel from a hefty bank account is misleading. You are my only true source of protection. I know that Your Word and Your wisdom will keep me from all kinds of harm. And the great thing is Your wisdom is free to all who ask. You pour it out on anyone who sincerely wants to know Your ways. Thank You for the protection that comes from knowing You and walking in Your ways. Teach me to trust in You alone for my security.

Healer

Be not wise in your own eyes; fear the LORD,
and turn away from evil. It will be healing to
your flesh and refreshment to your bones.
PROVERBS 3:7–8 ESV

Dear Father, when faced with illness, I become obsessed with finding the best doctors and the newest medicines and the latest technology. I spend hours on the internet, searching for answers. I know that innovations in the medical field are from You, and I thank You for the wise doctors and scientists who make healing possible. But let me never forget: You are the Healer. You are the Great Physician. I know You can work miracles in my body if You choose to. But even if You don't, I will praise You. I will trust You. I know that simply following You provides a lasting kind of healing and refreshment to body, mind, and spirit. Thank You for Your healing, Father.

Your Words

My son, be attentive to my words; incline your ear to my sayings. Let them not escape from your sight; keep them within your heart. For they are life to those who find them, and healing to all their flesh.
PROVERBS 4:20–22 ESV

Dear Father, though it's a lot for my limited human mind to comprehend, I know Your Word is not stagnant. It is a living, active thing and is profitable for every area of my life. Many times in the Bible, Your Word is referred to as a mystery. I'm grateful for modern medicine and all the wisdom You've provided through it. But I don't want to overlook the value of simply reading Your Word. I want to learn it, meditate on it, speak it, and make it a part of who I am. Your words are life. Your words are healing to my flesh. Draw me to Your Word, Father. Fill me with Your presence. I don't want to miss a bit of the amazing, abundant life You have for me.

A Soft Answer

A soft answer turns away wrath,
but a harsh word stirs up anger.
PROVERBS 15:1 ESV

Dear Father, I need help with some of my relationships. There are people in my life who make me angry and break my heart. I know I allow them to have far too much control over me. I think about our interactions and what I could have said or done differently. I lose sleep, worrying about how to make things right or how to put those people in their places. I know You want me to live peacefully with everyone, as much as it's up to me. But I need Your help, Lord. When I'm tempted to respond in anger or frustration, silence my tongue. Let the phone ring or the dog bark—anything to interrupt me before I say something I shouldn't. Fill my mouth with kind, encouraging words. Fill my heart with a genuine love for these people. Let all my interactions reflect You.

Gracious Words

Gracious words are like a honeycomb,
sweetness to the soul and health to the body.
PROVERBS 16:24 ESV

Dear Father, I can remember being taught "You catch more flies with honey than you do with vinegar." I know there's truth in that. But when others upset me or insult me or make me angry, I have a hard time speaking with honey. When I respond to others with anger or rudeness, it only makes things worse. Harsh words cause an already strained relationship to disintegrate even more. Teach me to speak only gracious words. I know that's the only way to bring healing to a relationship. Even if the association can't be mended, calm, sweet words will bring healing to my spirit. Kind, gracious speech flowing from my mouth will mend the broken parts in me. Fill me so much with Your love that it spills into all my interactions, even with difficult people.

Let God Handle It

*Do not say, "I will repay evil"; wait for
the LORD, and he will deliver you.*
PROVERBS 20:22 ESV

. . . .

Dear Father, You know the hurts I've endured. You know all about the people who have treated me poorly, gossiped about me, and acted with malice toward me. You know the name and address of every abuser, every liar and cheat who has hurt me. My first reaction when someone is cruel is to figure out a way to repay them. An eye for an eye, I say. At least, that's what my old human nature says. I know that's not how You want me to respond. It's really hard, Lord. But teach me to wait. Teach me to trust You. Teach me to keep pouring out Your love and grace, infusing every situation with Your presence and power. I know You will see justice happen. And I know You'll repay me for my faithful obedience. Give me patience, Lord. I leave it in Your hands.

Restored

*"For I will restore health to you, and your
wounds I will heal, declares the Lord."*
JEREMIAH 30:17 ESV

Dear Father, You created me. You know more about what's going on in my body than any scan or test can show. I'm frustrated when sickness keeps me from living the full, active life I want to live. But I trust You completely for my healing. I know You'll heal me when You're ready. It might be here on earth—and that's what I want. That's what I'm asking for, Lord. I want You to rid my body of this illness. Use whatever means You choose, whether it's a miraculous touch, a new technology, or a brilliant doctor. I want to be healed. But Father, I know Your ways are higher than my ways. If You choose to wait until heaven to heal me, I will rejoice in that too. I can't imagine the joys You have in store for me there. Give me grace to accept whatever healing You choose to give.

Lay It Down

*"Nevertheless, I will bring health and healing
to it; I will heal my people and will let them
enjoy abundant peace and security."*

JEREMIAH 33:6 NIV

. . . .

Dear Father, I'm a mess. So many areas of my life need Your healing touch. My body needs healing. My relationships need healing. Even my nation needs healing, Father. For everything that's sick, I know You are the source of health. You are the Great Physician. Right now, instead of obsessing and worrying over things I can't control, I bring them all to You. I lay them at Your feet, and I trust You for healing and peace. When I start to take them back, thinking I can do better than You can, remind me of who You are. Thank You for Your kindness, Your compassion, and Your love. I'm so glad You are my Healer.

Generous

"Bring the full tithe into the storehouse, that there may be food in my house. And thereby put me to the test, says the LORD of hosts, if I will not open the windows of heaven for you and pour down for you a blessing until there is no more need."

MALACHI 3:10 ESV

Dear Father, I know this verse isn't a formula for earthly wealth. You're more concerned about my heart than my finances. You are generous, and You made me in Your image. That means You want me to be generous too. You want me to give for the joy of giving, because that's why *You* give. Forgive me for holding so tightly to what's mine—things I wouldn't have without Your blessing in the first place. Let me feel the thrill of sharing. Make me excessively generous, as You are. I know You will reward that kind of attitude in ways I can't even imagine. Make me wise with my resources, and make me generous like You.

Subject Index

Everyday Concerns 7, 9, 11, 13, 15, 16, 17, 18, 21, 24, 25, 26, 29, 30, 34, 39, 42, 43, 44, 46, 47, 48, 51, 52, 53, 55, 58, 59, 60, 62, 65, 66, 67, 68, 69, 70, 71, 72, 77, 80, 82, 83, 85, 86, 88, 90, 92, 94, 97, 98, 100, 102, 103, 104, 107, 108, 109, 110, 111, 112, 113, 114, 115, 116, 117, 118, 121, 122, 123, 124, 125, 126, 127, 128, 129, 130, 131, 132, 133, 134, 135, 136, 137, 138, 139, 142, 145, 147, 149, 156, 157, 159, 160, 161, 162, 163, 164, 165, 166, 167, 169, 170, 174, 185

The Future 13, 14, 16, 17, 18, 21, 23, 24, 32, 33, 36, 37, 38, 39, 41, 43, 44, 45, 46, 47, 48, 49, 50, 51, 52, 53, 54, 55, 56, 58, 62, 66, 67, 68, 69, 71, 72, 74, 76, 77, 78, 79, 80, 81, 82, 83, 85, 86, 87, 89, 90, 91, 92, 93, 97, 98, 99, 100, 101, 102, 103, 108, 109, 110, 111, 112, 113, 114, 116, 117, 118, 122, 123, 124, 125, 126, 128, 129, 131, 132, 133, 135, 136, 137, 138, 139, 141, 142, 143, 144, 145, 147, 150, 151, 152, 153, 154, 156, 159, 160, 162, 163, 164, 165, 167, 168, 172, 185

Health 16, 17, 18, 24, 26, 31, 34, 38, 44, 45, 46, 54, 55, 56, 64, 67, 69, 72, 77, 85, 89, 92, 97, 98, 107, 108, 109, 110, 111, 112, 113, 121, 122, 128, 135, 137, 139, 142, 147, 149, 151, 152, 153, 154, 156, 159, 161, 162, 163, 164, 165, 168, 172, 175, 179, 180, 184, 185

Job Security 14, 16, 17, 18, 21, 26, 31, 35, 37, 44, 46, 55, 56, 57, 61, 67, 69, 72, 77, 85, 89, 91, 92, 97, 98, 109, 110, 111, 112, 113, 122, 128, 135, 137, 139, 142, 147, 148, 151, 152, 153, 154, 156, 159, 161, 162, 163, 164, 165, 176, 177, 178, 185

Money 14, 16, 17, 18, 21, 23, 31, 35, 37, 44, 46, 48, 55, 57, 62, 66, 67, 69, 72, 77, 85, 89, 91, 92, 97, 98, 106, 109, 110, 111, 112, 113, 122, 128, 135, 137, 138, 139, 142, 146, 147, 148, 151, 152, 153, 154, 156, 159, 161, 162, 163, 164, 165, 176, 177, 178, 185, 186

Relationships 8, 13, 16, 17, 18, 20, 25, 27, 28, 40, 44, 45, 46, 50, 54, 55, 58, 60, 61, 63, 66, 67, 69, 71, 72, 73, 75, 77, 85, 88, 89, 91, 92, 98, 105, 109, 110, 111, 112, 113, 118, 122, 126, 128, 129, 133, 134, 135, 137, 138, 139, 140, 142, 147, 151, 152, 153, 154, 156, 159, 161, 162, 163, 164, 165, 168, 181, 182, 183, 185

Self-Confidence 7, 8, 10, 12, 13, 16, 17, 18, 19, 20, 22, 25, 26, 29, 30, 36, 41, 42, 44, 46, 47, 48, 50, 51, 53, 54, 56, 62, 63, 64, 65, 67, 68, 70, 71, 80, 82, 83, 84, 89, 90, 91, 92, 96, 97, 98, 99, 101, 107, 108, 109, 110, 111, 112, 113, 114, 116, 118, 119, 120, 122, 126, 128, 130, 132, 133, 134, 135, 136, 139, 147, 149, 150, 151, 152, 153, 154, 155, 156, 157, 158, 159, 160, 164, 166, 167, 170, 171, 173, 174

About the Author

Renae Brumbaugh Green lives in Texas with her handsome, country-boy husband, two dogs, a bunch of chickens, and a duck. She teaches English and writing at Tarleton State University, writes a column for several newspapers, and writes books for children and grown-ups. In her free time, she does fun things with her young adult children, forces herself to exercise, reads historical fiction, and takes naps.

Dig into God's Word!

180 Bible Verses for Conquering Anxiety

This compact book pairs 180 Bible verses each with a devotional thought that is equal parts practical and encouraging. Here you'll find the strength to conquer your fears, as your heart is anchored to a solid foundation of faith.

Paperback / 978-1-64352-961-5

180 Bible Verses for a Less Stressed Life

This compact book pairs 180 Bible verses each with a devotional thought that is equal parts practical and encouraging. Here you'll find more peace and less stress, as your heart is anchored to a solid foundation of faith.

Paperback / 978-1-63609-246-1